VOLUME 3

THE
Afterlife
SERIES

Resurrection
& Judgment

WHAT AWAITS
THOSE WHO HAVE DIED

Don Stewart

Resurrection And Judgment

© 2015 By Don Stewart

Published by Educating Our World
www.educatingourworld.com
All rights reserved

English Versions Cited

The various English versions which we cite in this course, apart from the King James Version, all have copyrights. They are listed as follows.

TABLE OF CONTENTS

Resurrection and Judgement
(Volume 3 of 5)

In the first book of our series, "Living In The Light Of Eternity," we looked at some basic questions about death and dying. We found that death was not God's original intention for humanity. In fact, it only came about as a result of sin. We also discovered that death is not the end; it leads to an ultimate destination for every human being. Knowing this, we discussed how to live in the light of the eternity facing each of us.

In our next book, "What Happens One Second After We Die?" we learned that after people die their bodies go to the grave but their spirit or soul goes elsewhere. Indeed, they are either consciously in God's presence or in a place of punishment. This is known as the intermediate or "in-between" state.

However, by its very name, the intermediate, or the in-between, state has the idea that something is coming after that. Indeed, it is only temporary. This book will look at what comes after the "in-between" state.

In this third volume we will look at the subjects of the resurrection of the dead as well as the coming biblical judgments. The Bible says there will come a day when the bodies of the dead will be joined with their soul, their spirit. Once this occurs, the dead will be judged.

The righteous dead will not be judged for their sin. Judgment for believers consists of rewards. However, the same cannot be said for the unrighteous. Their judgment will consist of punishment.

The Bible has much to say about these topics. Therefore, it is crucial that we understand that one day our bodies will be raised and that we will be judged for our choices here upon the earth. Consequently, this is a very important topic to consider.

Does The Bible Directly Teach That The Dead Will Be Raised Someday?

The Bible says that when God created the first humans, Adam and Eve, He placed them in a perfect environment. They were perfect, everything in the world was perfect. In fact, God said the following about His finished creation.

> And God saw everything that he had made, and behold, it was very good. And there was evening and there was morning, the sixth day (Genesis 1:31 ESV).

Everything that God originally made was "very good." Yet this perfection did not last long. Scripture says that Adam and Eve disobeyed God and consequently the perfect world became imperfect.

Immediately after the first humans sinned in the Garden of Eden, the sentence of death was handed down to them as well as to their descendants. Previously, they had been warned about this.

> And the Lord God commanded the man, "You are free to eat from any tree in the garden; but you must not eat from the tree of the knowledge of good and evil, for when you eat from it you will certainly die (Genesis 2:16-17 NIV).

Death was now a reality. The death process had begun for Adam and Eve. Humanity then began to face the question, "Is there life after death?" The patriarch Job put it this way.

If a man dies, shall he live again? (Job 14:14 ESV).

Is death the end of everything or is there existence beyond this life? All of us, rich or poor, young or old, want to know the answer to this question.

THERE IS LIFE AFTER DEATH

The Bible answers this question loud and clear; the dead shall live again! Indeed, one of the great doctrines of the Christian faith is the resurrection of the dead. The Apostle Paul declared the following to the church at Rome.

> And even we Christians, although we have the Holy Spirit within us as a foretaste of future glory, also groan to be released from pain and suffering. We, too, wait anxiously for that day when God will give us our full rights as his children, including the new bodies he has promised us. Now that we are saved, we eagerly look forward to this freedom. For if you already have something, you don't need to hope for it (Romans 8:23,24 NLT).

Each believer is presently waiting for his or her new body that God has promised to give to every person who trusts in Jesus Christ as their Savior.

Though our earthly body dies, the spirit or soul never dies. The body ceases to function, but not the inner person, or spirit. Hence physical death does not end life; it is only one step in the ongoing and eternal process of conscious life.

THE DEAD ARE NOW IN THE IN-BETWEEN STATE

As we discovered from our previous book in this series, all of those who have died from the beginning of the world are presently in the intermediate or in-between state. They have moved from being alive on this earth to being alive in the unseen realm.

By definition, in-between means something has come before it and something will come afterward. What came before was life here upon this earth. What will come after the intermediate state is the resurrection of the dead. As we will see, everyone will be raised but not everyone will end up in the same place.

We need to make the following observations about one of the great doctrines of Scripture; the resurrection of the dead.

THERE ARE DIRECT STATEMENTS IN SCRIPTURE ABOUT THE RESURRECTION

The belief in the resurrection of the dead is progressively taught and illustrated in both testaments by direct statements. There is no doubt that those who lived in biblical times believed and taught that human existence did not end when a person died. We can make the following observations about the idea of the resurrection of the dead.

THE OLD TESTAMENT SPEAKS OF A RESURRECTION HOPE

The Old Testament speaks explicitly about a future resurrection for all who have died. They include the following testimonies by a number of different people spanning a long period of time.

THERE WAS HOPE FOR A RESURRECTION FOR JOB

The Bible tells the story of Job, a man who endured much grief and sorrow. In the midst of his suffering, Job made the following statement about the hope of a future resurrection.

> I know that my redeemer lives, and that in the end he will stand on the earth. And after my skin has been destroyed, yet in my flesh I will see God; I myself will see him with my own eyes—I, and not another. How my heart yearns within me (Job 19:25-27 NIV).

Although Job knew his body would be destroyed, he also had the promise that God would raise it again someday. Job had the belief in a personal resurrection.

HANNAH THE MOTHER OF SAMUEL BELIEVED THE DEAD WOULD RISE

Early in the history of Israel, at the time of the Judges, we find the hope expressed of the resurrection of the dead. Hannah, the mother of the prophet Samuel, believed there would be a future resurrection. Indeed, in her prayer to the Lord she acknowledged that He would one day raise the dead. She said.

> The LORD brings death and makes alive; he brings down to
> the grave and raises up (1 Samuel 2:6 NIV).

She had the hope of a future resurrection. The Lord would raise the dead back to life.

THE PSALMIST HAD HOPE OF A RESURRECTION

We find hope of a resurrection in the psalms. For example, we read the psalmist rejoicing in the following.

> No wonder my heart is filled with joy, and my mouth shouts
> his praises! My body rests in safety. For you will not leave my
> soul among the dead or allow your godly one to rot in the
> grave (Psalm 16:9,10 NLT).

The psalmist had hope for life beyond this life.

We find another example of the belief of a personal resurrection in another of the psalms. It says.

> As for me, I will see Your face in righteousness; I shall be
> satisfied when I awake in Your likeness (Psalm 17:15 NKJV).

This is a clear statement of the hope of a resurrection.

Later, in still another psalm, we read a further statement.

> But God will redeem my life from the grave; he will surely take me to himself (Psalm 49:15 NIV).

Again, there is the hope for the future resurrection of the body.

DANIEL THE PROPHET HAD HOPE FOR A NEW LIFE

The prophet Daniel realized that there was hope of a resurrection beyond the grave. He recorded it in this manner.

> Multitudes who sleep in the dust of the earth will awake: some to everlasting life, others to shame and everlasting contempt (Daniel 12:2 NIV).

Here we have another clear statement about the resurrection hope. The believer would be raised to everlasting life but the unbelievers to everlasting shame.

ZECHARIAH HAD HOPE FOR A RESURRECTION OF THE DEAD

There also seems to be a statement in Zechariah that refers to a future resurrection. He wrote the following.

> You will flee by my mountain valley, for it will extend to Azel. You will flee as you fled from the earthquake in the days of Uzziah king of Judah. Then the LORD my God will come, and all the holy ones with him (Zechariah 14:5 NIV).

If the "holy ones" is a reference to believers, then we have another statement of a future resurrection from an Old Testament prophet.

To sum up, we find the hope of the resurrection of the dead being directly taught in the Old Testament. From the earliest times, there was the hope of life beyond the grave.

THE NEW TESTAMENT DIRECTLY TAUGHT A RESURRECTION OF THE DEAD

We find this same truth taught in the New Testament. Indeed, there are a number of direct statements that teach the dead will rise.

JESUS TAUGHT THE DEAD WOULD BE RAISED

The Lord Jesus specifically taught that they dead would be raised. In John's gospel, we have the following statement of Christ recorded.

> For just as the Father raises the dead and gives them life, even so the Son gives life to whom he is pleased to give it (John 5:21 NIV).

Jesus said God the Father would give life to the dead. In the same manner, God the Son, Jesus Himself, will bring life to the dead.

Later, we find Jesus repeating this same truth. He said.

> Now this is the will of the one who sent me-that I should not lose one person of every one he has given me, but raise them all up at the last day (John 6:39 NET).

The dead in Christ will indeed be raised at a future time. This is the claim of Jesus.

At the grave of His friend Lazarus, Christ made it clear that He personally was the resurrection and the life. John records this astounding claim of Jesus.

> Jesus said to her, "I am the resurrection and the life. He who believes in Me, though he may die, he shall live" (John 11:25 NKJV).

There is no doubt that Jesus believed a resurrection would occur on the last day. Indeed, He would be the One who would raise the dead!

MARTHA, THE SISTER OF LAZARUS, BELIEVED THE DEAD WOULD RISE

Martha, the sister of Lazarus, believed in the resurrection of the dead. The gospel of John records it in this manner.

> Jesus said to her, "Your brother will rise again." Martha answered, "I know he will rise again in the resurrection at the last day (John 11:23,24 NIV).

We find from the statement of Martha that she believed there would be a time when the dead are raised. We should note that she was just an ordinary person; not a teacher of the Hebrew Scriptures.

Therefore, we discover that there was belief among the common people at the time of Christ of a resurrection from the dead.

THERE WAS EARLY PREACHING ABOUT THE RESURRECTION

We find the doctrine, or teaching, of the resurrection of believers was a part of the early preaching of the apostles. In the Book of Acts, the following is stated.

> They were greatly disturbed because the apostles were teaching the people and proclaiming in Jesus the resurrection of the dead (Acts 4:2 NIV).

The preaching of a future resurrection was part of the message of the apostles of Jesus. They linked the belief in a coming resurrection of the dead with the past resurrection of Jesus. Indeed, Jesus' resurrection assures a resurrection for those who believe in Him. This greatly disturbed the religious leaders since they were the ones who had caused Him to be put to death.

PAUL SPOKE OF THE RESURRECTION OF THE DEAD

The Book of Acts records the Apostle Paul, in certain historical situations, testifying to the resurrection of the dead. There was a group of religious leaders named the Pharisees who believed in the resurrection. A rival party, the Sadducees, did not believe in it to the same extent as the Pharisees. Both groups confronted the Apostle Paul. The following then occurred.

> Then Paul, knowing that some of them were Sadducees and the others Pharisees, called out in the Sanhedrin, "My brothers, I am a Pharisee, descended from Pharisees. I stand on trial because of the hope of the resurrection of the dead." When he said this, a dispute broke out between the Pharisees and the Sadducees, and the assembly was divided. (The Sadducees say that there is no resurrection, and that there are neither angels nor spirits, but the Pharisees believe all these things (Acts 23:6-8 NIV).

Paul was very specific about his belief of an actual resurrection from the dead. In fact, he told these religious leaders that this was the reason he was on trial.

The Apostle Paul later testified to his personal belief in a future resurrection of the dead. The Book of Acts records the following statement which he made.

> I am just as sure as these people are that God will raise from death everyone who is good or evil (Acts 24:15 CEV).

Again, the testimony of the resurrection came from the mouth of Paul. The righteous will be raised as well as the unrighteous.

PAUL WROTE EXTENSIVELY OF THE RESURRECTION FROM THE DEAD

Not only do we have the verbal testimony of Paul as recorded in the Book of Acts, there are passages in the writings of Paul in which the subject of the resurrection of the dead receives special treatment.

In one entire chapter, 1 Corinthians 15, Paul argues forcefully for the resurrection of the dead. He wrote that because Christ has risen from the dead, the believer will also rise someday. He put it this way to the Corinthians.

> But now Christ has come back from the dead. He is the very first person of those who have died to come back to life. Since a man brought death, a man also brought life back from death. As everyone dies because of Adam, so also everyone will be made alive because of Christ. This will happen to each person in his own turn. Christ is the first, then at his coming, those who belong to him will be made alive (1 Corinthians 15:20-23 God's Word).

Later in this chapter, Paul wrote further about the resurrection from the dead. He compared Jesus Christ to the first man, Adam. He wrote.

> So it is written: "The first man Adam became a living being"; the last Adam, a life-giving spirit. The spiritual did not come first, but the natural, and after that the spiritual. The first man was of the dust of the earth, the second man from heaven. As was the earthly man, so are those who are of the earth; and as is the man from heaven, so also are those who are of heaven. And just as we have borne the likeness of the earthly man, so shall we bear the likeness of the man from heaven (1 Corinthians 15:45-49 NIV).

We shall indeed someday "bear the likeness of the man from heaven." The bodily resurrection of the dead was a reality to Paul. He taught that Christ had risen from the grave and he also expected to be raised from the dead someday.

Paul speaks of the certainty of the resurrection of the dead in this passage to the Thessalonians.

> Brothers and sisters, we don't want you to be ignorant about those who have died. We don't want you to grieve like other people who have no hope. We believe that Jesus died and

came back to life. We also believe that, through Jesus, God will bring back those who have died. They will come back with Jesus. We are telling you what the Lord taught. We who are still alive when the Lord comes will not go into his kingdom ahead of those who have already died. The Lord will come from heaven with a command, with the voice of the archangel, and with the trumpet call of God. First, the dead who believed in Christ will come back to life. Then, together with them, we who are still alive will be taken in the clouds to meet the Lord in the air. In this way we will always be with the Lord. So then, comfort each other with these words (1 Thessalonians 4:13-18 God's Word).

Therefore, from the writings of Paul, we have many direct statements about the hope of the resurrection of the dead.

Consequently, we have no question whatsoever of his stance on this issue. To Paul, all of the dead are going to be raised someday.

JOHN ALSO WROTE OF THE RESURRECTION OF THE DEAD

John, the writer of the fourth gospel, three New Testament letters, as well as the Book of Revelation, also spoke of the resurrection. He wrote of a great coming event which he called "the first resurrection."

And I saw thrones, and they sat on them, and judgment was committed to them. Then I *saw* the souls of those who had been beheaded for their witness to Jesus and for the word of God, who had not worshiped the beast or his image, and had not received *his* mark on their foreheads or on their hands. And they lived and reigned with Christ for a thousand years. But the rest of the dead did not live again until the thousand years were finished. This *is* the first resurrection. Blessed and holy *is* he who has part in the first resurrection. Over such the second death has no power, but they shall be priests of

God and of Christ, and shall reign with Him a thousand years (Revelation 20:4-6 NKJV).

A resurrection of the dead is coming.

Hence the biblical writers looked forward to a day when the dead would rise. They were united in this belief.

CONCLUSION: BOTH TESTAMENTS DIRECTLY TEACH THE RESURRECTION OF THE DEAD

From the totality of the evidence, we find both testaments directly teaching the dead would someday return to life where their spirits, or souls, would join with their bodies. This coming resurrection includes both the righteous dead as well as the wicked dead.

SUMMARY TO QUESTION 1
DOES THE BIBLE DIRECTLY TEACH THAT THE DEAD WILL BE RAISED SOMEDAY?

The Bible says that death is not normal. God's original intention for humanity was life, not death. However, death entered the world because of sin. Presently the world is in a fallen state. Yet, after death there is still existence. Indeed, everyone who dies goes to one of two places: either to be with the Lord or to be separated from Him in a place of punishment.

Nevertheless, this is not our final destination; it is merely an intermediate or in-between state. The fact that it is intermediate means that something is going to come after that. What comes after the intermediate state is the resurrection of the dead!

The resurrection of the dead is something that is taught in both testaments. The great promise of Scripture is that one day the body will be re-united with the spirit. There will be a restoration of the entire person with both the body and the soul, or spirit. From a study of the Scripture there are a number of important facts that are clear.

To begin with, Scripture says that there will indeed be a resurrection of the dead. This is one of the main themes of the Bible. It is taught in the Old Testament but more fully developed in the New Testament. There is no doubt whatsoever that the dead will rise. God's Word says so in a number of direct statements.

We also learn that this resurrection will be universal; everyone will be raised. There will be no exceptions. God will raise the bodies of every human being who has ever lived.

While everyone who has ever lived will be raised, everyone will not go to the same destination. In fact, there will be an enormous difference in the character of the resurrection. There is a resurrection unto life and a resurrection unto death; a separation from God's holy presence and love. The resurrection will thus be a prelude to the final judgment of both the righteous and the wicked.

We also learn that those who are raised will never die again. Death will no longer have power over those who have been raised.

In sum, there will be a resurrection that leads to life and one that leads to punishment.

Does The Bible Symbolically Teach That The Dead Will Rise?

Not only do we find the Bible directly teaching that the dead will rise, there are passages in Scripture that symbolically speak of the resurrection of the dead. We can provide two examples.

1. ABRAHAM BELIEVED GOD WOULD RAISE ISAAC IF NECESSARY

God told the Old Testament character Abraham to sacrifice his son Isaac, the son of promise.

> Some time later, God tested Abraham's faith. "Abraham!" God called. "Yes," he replied. "Here I am." "Take your son, your only son—yes, Isaac, whom you love so much—and go to the land of Moriah. Go and sacrifice him as a burnt offering on one of the mountains, which I will show you (Genesis 22:1-2 NLT).

Yet Abraham knew that Isaac had to continue to live on to give Abraham descendants through him. Previously God had promised that his future descendants would come through Isaac.

> Then God said to Abraham, "Regarding Sarai, your wife— her name will no longer be Sarai. From now on her name will be Sarah. And I will bless her and give you a son from her! Yes, I will bless her richly, and she will become the mother of many nations. Kings of nations will be among her descendants (Genesis 17:15-16 NLT).

Hence Abraham said in faith to the men with him.

> Stay here with the donkey while I and the boy go over there. We will worship and then we will come back to you (Genesis 22:5 NIV).

The writer to the Hebrews comments upon this event. He wrote that Abraham had faith that the Lord would raise Isaac from the dead, if necessary. He said.

> Abraham believed that God could bring Isaac back from the dead. Abraham did receive Isaac back from the dead in a figurative sense (Hebrews 11:19 God's Word).

Although Abraham had been told by God to offer up his son Isaac as a sacrifice, he knew that Isaac would survive. Indeed, God had promised Abraham that he would have descendants through his son Isaac.

Therefore, Abraham concluded that God would have to raise Isaac back to life to fulfill His promise to the patriarch.

2. JONAH'S EXPERIENCE IS SYMBOLIC OF JESUS' RESURRECTION

The experience of the prophet Jonah was also symbolic of the resurrection of Jesus Christ. In fact, Jesus used him as illustrating the fact that He would rise from the dead. We read of the following confrontation between Jesus and the religious rulers of His day. Scripture says.

> Then some of the Pharisees and teachers of the law said to him, "Teacher, we want to see a sign from you." He answered, "A wicked and adulterous generation asks for a sign! But none will be given it except the sign of the prophet Jonah. For as Jonah was three days and three nights in the belly of a huge fish, so the Son of Man will be three days and three nights in the heart of the earth (Matthew 12:38-40 NIV).

Jonah's experience was symbolic of the resurrection of Jesus. According to Jesus, as Jonah was, so shall the Son of Man be. Jonah was three days in the belly of the great sea creature and Jesus would spend three days in the grave.

But as Jonah came out alive from the huge sea creature so Jesus will come back alive from the grave. In other words, there would be a resurrection of His body.

Therefore, we find the resurrection taught symbolically in the Scripture through Abraham's attempted sacrifice of Isaac and the account of Jonah and the huge sea creature.

SUMMARY TO QUESTION 2
DOES THE BIBLE SYMBOLICALLY TEACH THAT THE DEAD WILL RISE?

We discovered that the doctrine of the resurrection of the dead was taught by a number of direct statements in the Scripture. These truths are not only taught by direct statements, we also find that they are taught symbolically.

Through such historical episodes as Abraham taking his son Isaac to become a sacrifice, as well as the time the prophet Jonah spent in the stomach of the great sea creature, we find the resurrection symbolically pictured in these accounts.

They further illustrate the biblical belief that the dead will one day rise.

Is The Resurrection Of The Dead Taught By Predictive Prophecy?

By direct statements, as well as symbolically, the Bible teaches that the dead will someday be raised. In other words, this life leads to another destination.

In addition to direct statements and symbolism, we also find the doctrine of the resurrection of the dead taught through predictive prophecy. Both testaments predict the future resurrection of the dead. We find statements where the resurrection of the righteous and unrighteous will actually occur.

1. ISAIAH THE PROPHET

Isaiah the prophet wrote of a future resurrection of those who had died. He stated this hope in the resurrection as follows.

> But your dead will live, Lord; their bodies will rise—let those
> who dwell in the dust wake up and shout for joy—your dew
> is like the dew of the morning; the earth will give birth to her
> dead (Isaiah 26:19 NIV).

Consequently, he predicted a time when the dead would come back to life. Indeed, the dead corpses will rise.

2. HOSEA

The prophet Hosea also records the Lord saying that the dead will rise again. In this statement of the Lord, of victory over death, we read the following.

> I will ransom them from the power of the grave; I will redeem them from death. Where, O death, are your plagues? Where, O grave, is your destruction? I will have no compassion (Hosea 13:14 NIV).

Here is another prediction of the coming resurrection. The grave, we are told, does not ultimately destroy. The Lord will be victorious over it.

3. JESUS

The New Testament also predicts the future rising of the dead. Jesus spoke of it often. For example we read the following in the Gospel of Luke.

> But when you give a banquet, invite the poor, the crippled, the lame, the blind, and you will be blessed. Although they cannot repay you, you will be repaid at the resurrection of the righteous (Luke 14:13,14 NIV).

Our Lord believed that there would be a resurrection of the righteous.

In another place, He explained that those in the resurrected state neither marry nor are they given in marriage.

> But those who are counted worthy to take part in that age and in the resurrection from the dead neither marry nor are given in marriage. For they cannot die anymore, because they are like angels and are sons of God, since they are sons of the resurrection (Luke 20:35,36 HCSB).

Note that the Lord also said that those who are raised cannot die anymore. In other words, they are raised to everlasting life.

In another place, Christ said there would come a time when the dead would come out of their tombs. John records Him saying.

> Do not be amazed at this, for a time is coming when all who are in their graves will hear his voice and come out— those who have done what is good will rise to live, and those who have done what is evil will rise to be condemned (John 5:28,29 NIV).

Truly, Jesus taught that the resurrection of the dead was a future reality. There is certainly no doubt about this.

4. PAUL SPOKE OF A COMING RESURRECTION

In Athens, the Apostle Paul spoke about the coming resurrection. He put it this way when he spoke to a skeptical crowd.

> For he has set a day for judging the world with justice by the man he has appointed, and he proved to everyone who this is by raising him from the dead. When they heard Paul speak of the resurrection of a person who had been dead, some laughed, but others said, "We want to hear more about this later" (Acts 17: 31,32 NLT).

According to Paul, there will be a future resurrection of all who have died. Once they are raised, Jesus Christ will judge them.

Therefore, both testaments actually predict that there will be a time when the dead will be raised. Consequently, we also learn about the resurrection of the dead through predictive prophecy.

SUMMARY TO QUESTION 3
IS THE RESURRECTION OF THE DEAD TAUGHT BY PREDICTIVE PROPHECY?

From the teaching of the Bible we find that one of the major doctrines of the faith is the resurrection of the dead. There will indeed come a day when the bodies of the dead will be raised back to life. This is directly taught in Scripture.

As we also observed, the resurrection was taught symbolically in the examples of Abraham and Isaac as well as with Jonah the prophet.

The resurrection of the dead is also a predicted event. Indeed, the prophets in both testaments spoke of a day when the dead would rise. This was the hope that each of them had.

Because this doctrine is stated and restated, we find that the resurrection of the dead is an extremely important biblical teaching.

What Does Jesus' Resurrection Teach Us About The Future Resurrection Of The Dead?

The future resurrection of the human race is illustrated in the resurrection of Jesus Christ from the dead. Although the Bible records examples of God bringing people back to life, or resuscitating them, the resurrection of Jesus Christ was unique. This can be seen in a number of ways.

1. JESUS WAS THE FIRST TO RISE FROM THE DEAD

Paul testified that Jesus was the first to rise from the dead. In the Book of Acts the following statements of Paul are recorded for us.

> But I have had God's help to this very day, and so I stand here and testify to small and great alike. I am saying nothing beyond what the prophets and Moses said would happen— that the Christ would suffer and, as the first to rise from the dead, would proclaim light to his own people and to the Gentiles (Acts 26:22,23 NIV).

Jesus is the first to rise from the dead but He certainly will not be the last! Indeed, our Lord is the first of many who will rise.

We read about others who will come after him in Paul's letter to the Corinthians.

> Just as everyone dies because we all belong to Adam, everyone who belongs to Christ will be given new life. But there is

an order to this resurrection: Christ was raised as the first of the harvest; then all who belong to Christ will be raised when he comes back (1 Corinthians 15:22-23).

Therefore, many will be raised after Him.

2. JESUS DID NOT DIE AGAIN

It is important that we understand the uniqueness of Jesus' resurrection. While other people in the Bible were brought back to life after their death, they eventually died again. Jesus is the first biblical example of one who has been raised from the dead *never* to die again. Indeed, Jesus rose to die no more. Jesus himself testified to this fact.

I *am* He who lives, and was dead, and behold, I am alive forevermore. Amen. And I have the keys of Hades and of Death (Revelation 1:18 NKJV).

Jesus lives forevermore. Death has no authority over Him.

3. IT IS A PRELUDE TO JUDGMENT

It is also important to note that the resurrection of the body is always linked with judgment. Before people are judged in the afterlife, they are raised from the dead.

Therefore, the resurrection of the dead always happens before judgment, because judgment necessitates a resurrection of that person. The Scriptures always link the two.

We read about this in the Book of Hebrews. It says the following.

Therefore, leaving the elementary message about the Messiah, let us go on to maturity, not laying again the foundation of repentance from dead works, faith in God, teaching about ritual washings, laying on of hands, the resurrection of the dead, and eternal judgment (Hebrews 6:1,2 HCSB).

Consequently the resurrection of the dead and eternal judgment are inseparable. They are also basic, or foundational, beliefs of the Christian faith. In the remainder of this book we will explore in detail these two important doctrines; resurrection and judgment.

CONCLUSION: THE RESURRECTION OF THE BODY IS TAUGHT IN FOUR DIFFERENT WAYS IN SCRIPTURE

To sum up, the Bible, in both testaments, promises that the dead will rise again. The doctrine of the resurrection of the dead is both clear and precise. It is indeed one of the main teachings of Scripture.

As we have seen with our previous questions, this is done in four different ways.

1. BY DIRECT STATEMENTS

2. SYMBOLICALLY

3. THROUGH PREDICTIVE PROPHECY

4. BY THE RESURRECTION OF JESUS CHRIST

These are four different ways in which the Bible teaches that the dead will someday rise. Clearly, the resurrection of the dead is a central teaching of Scripture.

SUMMARY TO QUESTION 4
WHAT DOES JESUS' RESURRECTION TEACH US ABOUT THE FUTURE RESURRECTION OF THE DEAD?

In our previous three questions, we found that the resurrection was taught by direct statements, symbolically, as well as through predictive prophecy.

Finally, we discover that the resurrection of the dead is also seen through the resurrection of Jesus Christ. His resurrection guarantees the resurrection of the believer. He is the first of many to come back from the dead. While others have been brought back to life after their death, they eventually died again and this time they remained dead. When Christ rose from the dead, He rose never to die again.

In addition, we discover that the resurrection of the dead is always linked to judgment. After the dead are raised, they will be judged. In fact, the judgment of the dead necessitates a resurrection.

In sum, this life is certainly not all that there is. After death, we find that there is an in-between state where our spirits or souls live separately from our bodies.

However, a great day is coming. One day, the dead bodies of believers will be reunited with our spirits in a new glorious body, a resurrection body. This is the wonderful hope the Scripture proclaims for all of those who have believed in the God of the Bible.

How Do We Understand Certain Biblical Statements That Seemingly Deny The Resurrection Of The Dead?

In both testaments, the Bible clearly teaches that there will come a time when all people who have ever lived will be raised bodily from their graves. Jesus said.

> Don't be surprised at what I've just said. A time is coming when all the dead will hear his voice, and they will come out of their tombs. Those who have done good will come back to life and live. But those who have done evil will come back to life and will be judged (John 5:28,29 God's Word).

There will be an actual resurrection of all those who have died. This is the consistent teaching of Scripture. Everyone will be raised and then judged.

ARE THERE CONTRADICTORY PASSAGES?

There are, however, some passages in the Bible that seem to contradict the idea that the dead will be raised. The following statements in Scripture seem contradictory to the idea that the dead will come back to life in a new body. They are as follows.

1. THERE NO RETURN FROM THE GRAVE? (JOB 7:9)

In the Book of Job, we read a statement which says that the dead do not return. It states this as follows.

> As a cloud vanishes and is gone, so he who goes down to the grave does not return (Job 7:9 NIV).

This seems to say that death is the end. If this is the case, then there is no resurrection from the dead for anyone.

2. THOSE THAT SLEEP DO NOT RISE (JOB 14:12)

In another place in the Book of Job it also says that those who sleep in death will not awake. We read the following.

> So he lies down and does not rise; till the heavens are no more, people will not awake or be roused from their sleep (Job 14:12 NIV).

This statement seems to clearly contradict the idea of any resurrection of the dead.

3. THE DEAD DO NOT RISE (ISAIAH 26:14)

Isaiah the prophet also wrote about how the dead do not rise. He put it this way.

> They are now dead, they live no more; those departed spirits do not rise. You punished them and brought them to ruin; you wiped out all memory of them (Isaiah 26:14 NIV).

This is another seeming contradiction of the doctrine which is taught elsewhere that the dead will indeed rise.

4. THOSE THAT FALL WILL NOT RISE (AMOS 8:14)

In the Book of Amos, we read of those who have fallen in death. We are told that they will not rise up.

> How horrible it will be for those who swear by Ashimah, the idol of Samaria, and say, "I solemnly swear, Dan, as your god lives.... I solemnly swear as long as there is a road to

Beersheba...." Those who say this will fall and never get up again (Amos 8:14 God's Word).

There is no resurrection for them. They will never get up again.

WHAT DO THESE STATEMENTS MEAN?

How are we to understand these statements in light of the rest of Scripture which clearly teach the dead will be raised? Do these passages contradict what other parts of the Bible make clear; the dead will be bodily raised from the grave?

THERE IS NO CONFLICT WHEN PROPERLY UNDERSTOOD

When these passages are read in context, it will be seen that they are not in conflict with the rest of Scripture. Indeed, the Bible does not contradict itself since the ultimate author behind the books is God Almighty. We can make the following observations.

THE PASSAGES IN JOB MUST BE UNDERSTOOD IN CONTEXT

Before we look at the two passages in Job we mentioned, it is worth noting how we should evaluate these statements. In Job, we have the record of Job and his friends giving their opinion on Job's suffering. While they are doing this, they also make statements about such subjects as the afterlife. However, we must be careful how we understand these statements. Indeed, at the end of their discussion the Lord broke into the conversation with the following.

> Then the Lord answered Job from the whirlwind: "Who is this that questions my wisdom with such ignorant words (Job 38:1-2 NLT).

Therefore, we have the Lord's commentary on the various things said previously in the Book of Job. He calls them "ignorant words!"

Consequently, we need to be careful about quoting any part of these discussions and assuming Job and his friends are speaking biblical truth. The only way we can cite them as authoritative biblical teaching is if they say something which is elsewhere confirmed in Scripture as a direct teaching of the Lord. Otherwise, we should be skeptical about their statements.

1. JOB 7:9 DOES NOT DENY THE RESURRECTION

In context, this passage in the Book of Job is not denying the resurrection of the dead. In fact, the next verse reads as follows.

> He will never come to his house again; his place will know him no more (Job 7:10 NIV).

The person who dies will not return to his house again. Those who die cannot return to the same body that died. This is consistent with what the Scripture teaches with respect to the resurrection. Paul wrote.

> For this corruptible must be clothed with incorruptibility, and this mortal must be clothed with immortality (1 Corinthians 15:53 HCSB).

Those that die have to have a new body; the old one perishes. Therefore, this statement is consistent with the rest of biblical teaching that the dead cannot come back in exactly the same body that died.

2. JOB 14:12 SPEAKS OF THE RESURRECTION AT THE END OF TIME

This statement does not deny the resurrection; it merely says that the resurrection will occur at the end of time. This is consistent with other parts of Scripture. Daniel wrote.

> At that time Michael, the great prince who protects your people, will arise. There will be a time of distress such as has not happened from the beginning of nations until then. But at that time your people—everyone whose name is found written in the book—will be delivered. Multitudes who sleep in the dust of the earth will awake: some to everlasting life, others to shame and everlasting contempt (Daniel 12:1,2 NIV).

The resurrection will indeed come, but not until the end of time. Until that time the bodies of the dead will remain in the grave. Therefore, we do not have a contradiction here.

3. ISAIAH 26:14 SAYS PEOPLE WON'T LIVE AGAIN UNTIL THE RESURRECTION

Isaiah the prophet is certainly not denying the biblical doctrine of resurrection of the dead. In fact, a couple of verses further down he says the following.

> But your dead will live; their bodies will rise. You who dwell in the dust, wake up and shout for joy. Your dew is like the dew of the morning; the earth will give birth to her dead (Isaiah 26:19 NIV).

Isaiah is affirming that these people will not live again on the earth until the resurrection. He is not denying the resurrection of the dead.

4. AMOS 8:14 SAYS THAT GOD'S DEAD ENEMIES WILL NOT HURT THE PEOPLE AGAIN

The passage in Amos has to do with the enemies of God who are killed. They will never rise up and hurt God's people again. The idea is that the enemies of God are dead and will stay dead. The resurrection of the dead is not the subject that is being dealt with in this context.

Therefore, when these statements are understood in their context, there is no contradiction with the biblical doctrine of the resurrection. Consequently, we can confidently assert that there will come a day when the dead are raised; just as the Bible says.

THERE ARE SIMILAR STATEMENTS IN ECCLESIASTES

We should also note that in the Old Testament book of Ecclesiastes there are a number of statements which also seem to contradict what the Scripture says about the afterlife and the resurrection of the dead.

In the next book of our series, *Heaven*, we have a question about these statements in Ecclesiastes. In it, we go into some detail about this particular Old Testament book and the statements it makes about the afterlife. At the end of the day, we will discover that there are no contradictions about the biblical teaching of the afterlife when these passages are properly understood.

SUMMARY TO QUESTION 5
HOW DO WE UNDERSTAND CERTAIN BIBLICAL STATEMENTS THAT SEEMINGLY DENY THE RESURRECTION OF THE DEAD?

At first glance, there are a few passages in the Old Testament which seem to teach that those who are dead will not rise. If this is the case then we would have the biblical authors contradicting themselves. Indeed, there are many clear statements about a coming resurrection. How are we to understand these so-called contradictions?

Although there are some passages in the Old Testament that may seem to contradict the biblical teaching of the resurrection of the dead, further study shows this is not the case. Each of these passages can be understood in harmony with the rest of the Scripture, which clearly teaches that there will come a day when the dead will be raised. The Bible is therefore consistent in its teaching from beginning to end; the dead will rise someday.

To begin with, we mentioned that the passages in the Book of Job need to be carefully examined. Indeed, the Lord called their discussion "ignorant words." Therefore, we need to be careful in citing any of their statements. Yet it seems that in context that these people were not necessarily denying a resurrection from the dead.

For example, there is a statement in Job that says there is no return from the grave. However, this is talking about any return in this life. It does not contradict the idea of a resurrection.

In Job, it also says that those who sleep in the grave do not rise. Yet this is again speaking of those living upon the earth; they will not come back to life on the earth. It says nothing about a future resurrection.

Isaiah the prophet was not denying the resurrection of the dead. Indeed, a few verses later he emphasized that the dead would rise. He was merely saying that the dead would no longer live in this life here upon the earth. He was not dealing with the afterlife but rather what will take place in this life.

In the Book of Amos, it says God's enemies won't rise up and hurt them again. This is speaking of this life, not the next life. Again, we have no contradiction about the doctrine of a resurrection from the dead.

In sum, the resurrection of the dead is a major doctrine in the Bible. When examined in context no passage of Scripture contradicts this important biblical truth.

QUESTION 6

Who Will Raise The Dead?

The Bible teaches the resurrection of the dead. In other words, this life is not the end as far as humans are concerned. After death we have an ultimate destination. The dead will be eventually be raised.

Scripture also clearly tells us who it is that will bring the dead back to life. We can make the following observations about what the Scripture says.

1. GOD WILL RAISE THE DEAD

The Bible says that the God of the Bible, and no one else, is the One who will raise the dead. The psalmist wrote.

> But God will redeem my life from the grave; he will surely take me to himself (Psalm 49:15 NIV).

God will be the One.

Paul in citing the Old Testament, said the following

> As it is written: "I have made you a father of many nations." He is our father in the sight of God, in whom he believed— the God who gives life to the dead and calls into being things that were not (Romans 4:17 NIV).

The God of the Bible is the only One capable of raising the dead. He gives life where there is no life.

2. THE TRINITY WILL RAISE THE DEAD

The Bible also makes it clear that each of the members of the Holy Trinity, God the Father, God the Son, and God the Holy Spirit, will be involved in the resurrection of the dead. The evidence can be seen as follows.

A. GOD THE FATHER WILL RAISE THE DEAD

Jesus said that God the Father will raise the dead. The gospel of John records Him saying the following about who it is who gives life to the deceased.

> And just as the Father raises the dead and gives them life, so the Son also gives life to anyone He wants to (John 5:21 HCSB).

Jesus said God the Father will bring the dead back to life.

B. GOD THE SON

God the Son, Jesus Christ, also participates in the resurrection. We read the following statement of Jesus as recorded in John's gospel.

> For this is the will of my Father-for everyone who looks on the Son and believes in him to have eternal life, and I will raise him up at the last day (John 6:40 NET).

The Son will also bring the dead back to life. Note that Jesus personally claimed to be the One who would do this supernatural feat.

C. GOD THE HOLY SPIRIT

The Third Person of the Trinity, God the Holy Spirit, will also be part of the resurrection process. The Apostle Paul wrote the following to the Romans about the participation of the Holy Spirit in the resurrection of Christ.

> But if the Spirit of Him who raised Jesus from the dead dwells in you, He who raised Christ from the dead will also give life to your mortal bodies through His Spirit who dwells in you (Romans 8:11 NKJV).

The Spirit which brought Jesus back from the dead, the Holy Spirit, will also someday raise up those of us who believe in Him.

Therefore, we find that each member of the Godhead will be personally involved in the resurrection of the dead.

THIS IS FURTHER EVIDENCE OF THE DOCTRINE OF THE TRINITY

Interestingly, we have this statement from the Apostle Paul which he gave in his own defense.

> I'm on trial now because I expect God to keep the promise that he made to our ancestors. Our twelve tribes expect this promise to be kept as they worship with intense devotion day and night. Your Majesty, the Jews are making accusations against me because I expect God to keep his promise. Why do all of you refuse to believe that God can bring dead people back to life (Acts 26:8 God's Word).

We have seen that the Father, the Son, and the Holy Spirit will all participate in the resurrection of the dead. Yet, here Paul says that God is the One who brings dead people back to life.

What is the inference from all of this? Well, if only God can bring the dead back to life, and the Bible says that the Father, the Son, and the Holy Spirit all participate in the resurrection of the dead, then the logical inference is that the Father, Son, and Holy Spirit are the One God. In other words, this is another illustration of the biblical teaching of the doctrine of the Trinity.

In sum, it is the united testimony of Scripture that the God of the Bible will raise the dead back to life. We are also specifically told that each individual member of the Trinity will be involved in this process.

SUMMARY TO QUESTION 6
WHO WILL RAISE THE DEAD?

The Bible says that the dead will be raised. There is no doubt about this. Scripture also says that the God of the Bible will do this.

As we examine the Word of God we find that each member of the Holy Trinity, God the Father, God the Son, Jesus Christ, and God the Holy Spirit will each be personally involved in our future resurrection.

Jesus that God the Father will someday raise the dead. Yet, in another place, our Lord said He Himself will bring the dead back to life.

In addition, the Apostle Paul wrote that the third Person of the Trinity, the Holy Spirit, will also be involved in the resurrection of those who have died.

Consequently, the resurrection of believers will take place with all three members of the Trinity being intimately involved.

We can also add something else to this. When Paul was giving his defense he emphasized that it is God who raises the dead!

Now, we have seen that the Father, the Son, and the Holy Spirit will each be involved in the future resurrection of the dead. If it is only God who raises the dead, then the logical conclusion is that the Father, Son, and Holy Spirit are the One God.

This, of course, is consistent with the totality of the teaching of Scripture about the nature of God. There is one God who exists, but He exists in three distinct persons, or centers of consciousness, God the Father, God the Son, and God the Holy Spirit. Simply stated, this is the doctrine of the Trinity.

Why Do Believers Need
A Resurrected Body?

The Bible says that believers will receive a new body upon their resurrection from the dead. Why is this necessary? Why do we need a resurrected body?

Scripture says that there are two basic reasons why this is so. They are as follows.

1. WE HAVE A BODY OF DEATH, A DYING BODY

The present body that we have is called in Scripture a body of death, or a dying body. Paul explained it this way to the Romans.

> What a wretched man I am! Who will rescue me from this dying body (Romans 7:24 HCSB).

Although the body was originally made perfect, sin has marred its perfection. The result for the human race is death and dying. This sinful body cannot last forever. It has to be replaced with a new body because we presently reside in a body of death.

2. WE NEED TO BE CHANGED TO BE IN THE PRESENCE OF GOD

There is another reason as to why believers need a new body. We cannot enter into God's holy presence in these sinful bodies. We need to be changed. A few important points need to be made.

A. GOD DWELLS IN UNAPPROACHABLE LIGHT

God lives in a state that is inaccessible for humans. Paul wrote to Timothy about how the Lord dwells in light unapproachable. He said.

> The only one who has immortality dwelling in unapproachable light, whom none of mankind has seen or can see, to who be honor and eternal might (1 Timothy 6:16 HCSB).

The translation, God's Word, puts it this way.

> He is the only one who cannot die. He lives in light that no one can come near. No one has seen him, nor can they see him. Honor and power belong to him forever! Amen (1 Timothy 6:16 God's Word).

God is holy. We are not. To be allowed in God's divine presence, our sinful bodies must be changed. This is essential.

B. SINFUL BODIES CANNOT INHERIT GOD'S KINGDOM

Our sinful bodies of flesh and blood cannot inherit God's kingdom. The Bible says that only the pure can see God. Jesus said.

> Blessed are the pure in heart: for they shall see God (Matthew 5:8 KJV).

The Apostle Paul also stressed the fact that flesh and blood, or sinful humans, cannot inherit God's kingdom. He wrote to the Corinthians and said.

> What I am saying, dear brothers and sisters, is that flesh and blood cannot inherit the Kingdom of God. These perishable bodies of ours are not able to live forever (1 Corinthians 15:50 NLT).

These perishable bodies have not been made for eternity. Indeed, our bodies must be changed.

The psalmist wrote something similar; only the pure can enter into God's presence. He explained it in this manner.

> Who may ascend the hill of the LORD? Who may stand in his holy place? He who has clean hands and a pure heart, who does not lift up his soul to an idol or swear by what is false (Psalm 24:3,4 NIV).

These qualifications certainly rules out all of us; none of us can meet these requirements! None of us have clean hands.

The Apostle John also wrote about the necessity of the believer being changed. He stated it in this manner.

> Beloved, now we are children of God; and it has not yet been revealed what we shall be, but we know that when He is revealed, we shall be like Him, for we shall see Him as He is. And everyone who has this hope in Him purifies himself, just as He is pure (1 John 3:2,3 NKJV).

For these reasons, it is necessary for our bodies to be changed when we enter into the Lord's presence. Therefore, we need a new body at the time of the resurrection of the dead.

SUMMARY TO QUESTION 7
WHY DO BELIEVERS NEED A RESURRECTED BODY?

The Bible says that believers will have to have new bodies before we can enter into the presence of the Lord. There are two basic reasons as to why this is so.

First, the bodies that we now have will not last forever. All of us are aware of this fact. Sin has marred their original perfection. They are in the process of deteriorating. Hence a change is in order.

Furthermore, to stand in the presence of a holy God, our sinful bodies must be changed. Nothing sinful or imperfect can remain in

God's perfect presence. Indeed, only perfection can be in the presence of our perfect God.

Consequently, these sinful, imperfect bodies must be changed to perfect bodies which are fit to be in His presence.

These are the two reasons as to why believers need a resurrected body.

Are There Some People Who Will Never Die? (The Rapture Of The Church)

Since the fall of humanity in the Garden of Eden, the normal experience for each human has been death. The sin of Adam and Eve brought death to the rest of us. The writer to the Hebrews stated the general truth in this manner.

> And just as people are appointed to die once, and then to face judgment (Hebrews 9:27 NET).

The statement that "it is appointed for people to die once" is one of those biblical statements which everyone, believer or unbeliever, can agree with. Death is the usual experience for fallen humanity. Humans will eventually meet their Maker by way of death.

THERE WERE TWO PEOPLE WHO DID NOT DIE

As we read through the pages of the Old Testament, we find this truth emphasized. Death is the norm for human beings.

There were, however, two exceptions to this rule; Enoch and Elijah. Neither of these men died.

1. ENOCH DID NOT DIE

The Bible says that Enoch, one of the earliest biblical characters, did not experience death like everyone else.

The Bible describes his fate in this manner.

> He enjoyed a close relationship with God throughout his life. Then suddenly, he disappeared because God took him (Genesis 5:24 NLT).

He was taken by the Lord before he died. This godly man simply disappeared.

The writer to the Hebrews explained it this way.

> Faith enabled Enoch to be taken instead of dying. No one could find him, because God had taken him. Scripture states that before Enoch was taken, God was pleased with him (Hebrews 11:5 God's Word).

Thus, this godly man never experienced death.

2. ELIJAH WENT INTO HEAVEN IN A WHIRLWIND

There is a second Old Testament figure which did not die, Elijah. Scripture says that he was brought into the presence of the Lord by means of a whirlwind.

We read in the Book of Kings.

> As they were walking along and talking together, suddenly a chariot of fire and horses of fire appeared and separated the two of them, and Elijah went up to heaven in a whirlwind (2 Kings 2:11 NIV).

Elijah was miraculously ushered into the presence of God.

A MYSTERY IS REVEALED: NOT EVERYONE WILL DIE

Not only are Enoch and Elijah the exception to the normal rule about death, the New Testament reveals to us something that had not been foretold; there will be a generation of people who will never die.

However, this future generation will experience something that Enoch and Elijah did not. Indeed, they will receive a glorified body!

PAUL WROTE TO THE THESSALONIANS ABOUT A MYSTERY

The Apostle Paul wrote to the church of Thessalonica about a mystery, a sacred secret, which had not been previously revealed. He said that before Jesus Christ returns to earth there will be an event known as the "rapture" of the church. The Scripture explains it in the following manner.

> Brothers and sisters, we do not want you to be uninformed about those who sleep in death, so that you do not grieve like the rest of mankind, who have no hope. For we believe that Jesus died and rose again, and so we believe that God will bring with Jesus those who have fallen asleep in him. According to the Lord's word, we tell you that we who are still alive, who are left until the coming of the Lord, will certainly not precede those who have fallen asleep. For the Lord himself will come down from heaven, with a loud command, with the voice of the archangel and with the trumpet call of God, and the dead in Christ will rise first. After that, we who are still alive and are left will be caught up together with them in the clouds to meet the Lord in the air. And so we will be with the Lord forever. Therefore encourage one another with these words (1 Thessalonians 4:13-18 NIV).

Those believers who are alive at this time will be caught up to meet the Lord in the air. They will not have to experience death. In addition, something else will happen to them.

As they are being caught up, their bodies will be changed from mortal to immortal. The catching up is called "the rapture" while the changing of their mortal bodies, into a glorified body, is also known as the "translation of the church."

HE TOLD THE CORINTHIANS ABOUT THE CHANGE THAT WILL OCCUR

Another explanation is given in First Corinthians. Paul wrote the following about the change that will occur in the body of these believers.

> But let me tell you a wonderful secret God has revealed to us. Not all of us will die, but we will all be transformed. It will happen in a moment, in the blinking of an eye, when the last trumpet is blown. For when the trumpet sounds, the Christians who have died will be raised with transformed bodies. And then we who are living will be transformed so that we will never die. For our perishable earthly bodies must be transformed into heavenly bodies that will never die. When this happens—when our perishable earthly bodies have been transformed into heavenly bodies that will never die—then at last the Scriptures will come true: "Death is swallowed up in victory. O death, where is your victory? O death, where is your sting?" For sin is the sting that results in death, and the law gives sin its power. How we thank God, who gives us victory over sin and death through Jesus Christ our Lord! So, my dear brothers and sisters, be strong and steady, always enthusiastic about the Lord's work, for you know that nothing you do for the Lord is ever useless (1 Corinthians 15:51-58 NLT).

A change will take place in these believers. They will go from mortal bodies to immortal bodies, from perishable to imperishable. They will not have to suffer death and a resurrection from the dead. Instead they will be instantly changed while alive.

OBSERVATIONS ON THESE PASSAGES

From these passages we can make the following observations about the exceptions to the general rule that everyone dies.

1. HE WANTS US TO UNDERSTAND THIS TRUTH

To begin with, Paul tells the Thessalonians that he wants us to understand the truth of the rapture of the church. This means it is something which we are able to understand. Indeed, it has not been hidden from us. Consequently, we should seek to comprehend what the Scripture teaches about this coming event.

2. THE TRUTH HE IS TEACHING IS GOD'S WORD

In addition, he said to the Thessalonians that this teaching on the rapture is the "Word of the Lord." In other words, what he is teaching is divine revelation, not his own opinion. This, of course, means that we should pay the utmost attention to what he has written.

3. THE TRUTH REVEALED: NOT EVERYONE WILL DIE

The mystery now revealed is as follows. Although death has been the norm for humanity, the Old Testament recorded two prominent exceptions, Enoch and Elijah.

We now learn that there will be many more. Indeed, an entire living generation of Christians will not experience death, but will be taken up to meet the Lord.

4. SOME WILL HAVE NO NEED OF A RESURRECTION

Those believers, who are living at the time of the rapture of the church, will not have to be resurrected. They will be changed, while they are alive, from mortal to immortal, from corruptible to incorruptible. They will be given a glorified body but not a resurrected body.

5. THEY WILL IMMEDIATELY MEET JESUS CHRIST

Certain people, whom the Lord raptures, will immediately be with Him in their changed bodies; there will be no waiting period. One moment they will be here upon the earth and the next moment they will be in the presence of the Lord.

6. THEY WILL BE WITH JESUS CHRIST FOREVER

These particular believers will be with Jesus Christ forever; never to be separated from Him. Such will be the unique experience of these Christians.

Therefore, dying is not the only way that people will get to heaven or to receive a new body. Many will receive their new body without having to die.

7. WE ARE TO COMFORT ONE ANOTHER WE THESE TRUTHS

The truths which Paul revealed are to be a source of comfort for believers. The dead are presently in a state of bliss waiting for the resurrection while the living believers will be instantaneously changed when the rapture occurs. When this event takes place there will be a great reunion of all believers in Christ, both past and present.

These are some of the important truths concerning the important doctrine of the rapture of the church.

Since the rapture of the church is such a crucial teaching we have devoted an entire book to this subject, "The Rapture."

SUMMARY TO QUESTION 8
ARE THERE SOME PEOPLE WHO WILL NEVER DIE? (THE RAPTURE OF THE CHURCH)

The resurrection from the dead will be the experience of most believers. The bodies of the dead will be re-united with their spirits.

However, a small number, in comparison, will not die but will be changed. Thus, there will be certain people who will never have to die to receive their glorified body.

This event is known as the "rapture" of the church. This will be similar, but not exactly the same, as to what happened in the case with the Old Testament characters Enoch and Elijah. Neither of these men died.

When this event occurs, the bodies of these believers will be changed from mortal to immortal, from a perishable body to one that does not perish. They will be with Jesus Christ immediately upon this transformation and will remain with Him forever. These believers will not have to experience death or the resurrection from the dead.

This event constitutes a genuine hope for all an entire generation of believers; they will never have to die. Furthermore, this event could occur at any time!

Consequently, we are to comfort one another with the fact that the dead believers will be raised and those who are alive at this time will meet them in the air by means of the rapture of the church. They too will be changed to a body that is incorruptible and immortal. These are indeed comforting truths!

What Will The Glorified Bodies Of The Righteous Be Like?

The Bible says those who have trusted the promises of God are going to be given a new body; one that will never die. The resurrection of Jesus Christ is the basis for our future resurrection. Paul wrote.

> But the fact is that Christ has been raised from the dead. He has become the first of a great harvest of those who will be raised to life again (1 Corinthians 15:20 NLT).

Jesus Christ was the first to come back from the dead, never to die again but there will be many more which follow.

THERE WILL BE A RESURRECTION OF THE BODY

There have been some who have objected to the idea of a literal resurrection of the dead. However, the Bible is clear on this matter. Simply stated, if the dead do not rise, then Jesus Christ did not rise from the dead. Paul wrote.

> If there is no resurrection of the dead, then not even Christ has been raised. And if Christ has not been raised, our preaching is useless and so is your faith (1 Corinthians 15:13 NIV).

Though the phrase "resurrection of the body" does not occur in the New Testament, the teaching is very clear. The Bible indicates that the bodies of believers will be changed. In fact, Scripture itself raises the question as to the nature of the resurrected body.

> But someone will say, "How are the dead raised up? And with what body do they come?" (1 Corinthians 15:35 NKJV).

There is no doubt that the Bible teaches the resurrection of the literal body of believers.

WHAT WILL THE RESURRECTION BODY WILL BE LIKE?

The Bible says a number of things about this glorified body that the righteous will receive. They include the following.

1. THE NEW BODIES WILL BE GOD-GIVEN

To begin with, God is the One who will give these new bodies to us. In other words, our new bodies will be of divine origin. Paul said the following to the Corinthians.

> Then God gives it a new body—just the kind he wants it to have (1 Corinthians 15:38 NLT).

The bodies of the dead will be changed into something new and wonderful.

2. THE BODY WILL BE SIMILAR TO THE RESURRECTED CHRIST

The resurrected body of the believer will, in some ways, be like the resurrected body of Jesus Christ. John said.

> Dear friends, we are God's children now, and what we will be has not yet been revealed. We know that when He appears, we will be like Him because we will see Him as He is (1 John 3:2 HCSB).

Scripture says that we will be like Him in a number of ways.

Paul wrote about how our bodies will be like His body; powerful and glorious. He wrote the following to the Philippians.

He will take these weak mortal bodies of ours and change them into glorious bodies like his own, using the same mighty power that he will use to conquer everything, everywhere (Philippians 3:21 NLT).

Thus, the new body will be similar to the body of the resurrected Christ.

3. THEY WILL BE LITERAL BODIES

The resurrection of believers will be just like that of Christ when He came back from the dead. In other words, we will have a literal body. The New Testament makes it clear that the body of Jesus was a real body. We read in John's gospel how Jesus told Thomas to touch His resurrected body. John wrote.

Then Jesus said to Thomas, "Put your finger here, and look at my hands. Take your hand, and put it into my side. Stop doubting, and believe" (John 20:27 God's Word).

On another occasion, He told His disciples that He had a genuine body. Luke writes Jesus saying the following.

Look at my hands. Look at my feet. You can see that it's really me. Touch me and make sure that I am not a ghost, because ghosts don't have bodies, as you see that I do! (Luke 24:39 NLT).

Jesus emphasized that His resurrected body was real. He was not a ghost.

As the resurrection body of Jesus Christ was literal, so will be the resurrected bodies of believers. Paul wrote the following to the Romans.

If the Spirit of him who raised Jesus from the dead dwells in you, he who raised Christ Jesus from the dead will also give life to your mortal bodies through his Spirit who dwells in you (Romans 8:11 ESV).

Consequently, we will receive a new body for all eternity.

4. THE BODIES WILL HAVE NEW CAPACITIES

The resurrected body of Jesus Christ had certain characteristics that we should note. The body was real, visible, capable of being handled, and recognizable. Yet at the same time it was able to pass through solid objects and disappear.

For example, we find that Jesus' body was able to suddenly appear in a locked room. We read about this in the gospel of John.

> On the evening of that day, the first day of the week, the disciples had gathered together and locked the doors of the place because they were afraid of the Jewish leaders. Jesus came and stood among them and said to them, "Peace be with you (John 20:19 NET).

Jesus suddenly appeared in their midst.

This miraculous event happened again a week later as John reports.

> After eight days His disciples were indoors again, and Thomas was with them. Even though the doors were locked, Jesus came and stood among them. He said, "Peace to you" (John 20:26 HCSB).

Jesus again miraculously appeared in their midst with the doors locked. He was able to move from the unseen world to our visible world in His resurrected body.

We find something similar happening earlier on Easter Sunday. Jesus was with two disciples in the village of Emmaus whose eyes had been supernaturally restrained from recognizing Him.

> While he was at the table with them, he took bread and blessed it. He broke the bread and gave it to them. Then their eyes were opened, and they recognized him. But he vanished from their sight (Luke 24:30,31 God's Word).

Jesus just vanished. He disappeared before their eyes! Believers will have similar capacities in their new body.

5. THEY WILL BE POWERFUL

The resurrected body of the believer will be powerful. They will never grow tired, never become weak, never age. Paul emphasized this when he wrote to the Corinthians.

> It is sown in dishonor; it is raised in glory. It is sown in weakness; it is raised in power (1 Corinthians 15:43 ESV).

Our mortal bodies are weak. This will not be the case with our resurrection bodies. They will be vastly superior to our earthly bodies in every conceivable way.

6. THE BODIES WILL BE DIFFERENT FROM ONE ANOTHER

While all believers will be given a glorified body, these bodies of the righteous will be different from one another. Paul compared our new bodies to the stars; each one is unique. He wrote.

> The sun has one kind of splendor, the moon has another kind of splendor, and the stars have still another kind of splendor. Even one star differs in splendor from another star. That is how it will be when the dead come back to life (1 Corinthians 15:41,42 God's Word).

Our bodies will not all look alike. We will be distinct.

7. WE WILL HAVE OUR SAME IDENTITY

At the resurrection, we will each keep our own unique identity. Paul wrote about this to the Corinthians. He said.

> And God both raised up the Lord and will also raise us up by His power (1 Corinthians 6:14 NKJV).

He will raise "us" up. This shows that we will each keep our unique individuality in the afterlife.

8. THOUGH OUR BODIES WILL BE TRANSFORMED OUR NEW BODIES WILL HAVE SOME CONTINUITY WITH THE OLD

Our new body will be a transformation of the old body. In other words, it will not be entirely new. There will be some type of connection between the natural body and the resurrection body.

However the material identity will not be exactly the same. The key issue is not so much material identity but of individuality; our memory and personality. These are the things that make up the unique identity of each of us.

Therefore, the body that will be raised is somehow related to the one that died. Paul wrote to the Corinthians.

> But someone may ask, "How will the dead be raised? What kind of bodies will they have?" What a foolish question! When you put a seed into the ground, it doesn't grow into a plant unless it dies first. And what you put in the ground is not the plant that will grow, but only a bare seed of wheat or whatever you are planting. Then God gives it the new body he wants it to have. A different plant grows from each kind of seed (1 Corinthians 15:35-38 NLT).

Consequently, like a seed planted in the ground, there is continuity between our present bodies and the future resurrection bodies we will receive.

9. THE CHANGE WILL BE INSTANTANEOUS FOR THE LIVING AND THE DEAD

Paul then emphasized that our change, or transformation, into the new body will be instantaneous. This is true whether we are alive or dead. He emphasized this to the Corinthians.

It will happen in a moment, in the blinking of an eye, when the last trumpet is blown. For when the trumpet sounds, the Christians who have died will be raised with transformed bodies. And then we who are living will be transformed so that we will never die. For our perishable earthly bodies must be transformed into heavenly bodies that will never die (1 Corinthians 15:52,53 NLT).

The same truth was taught to the Thessalonians. We read.

For the Lord himself will come down from heaven with a shout of command, with the voice of the archangel, and with the trumpet of God, and the dead in Christ will rise first. Then we who are alive, who are left, will be suddenly caught up together with them in the clouds to meet the Lord in the air. And so we will always be with the Lord (1 Thessalonians 4:17,18 NET).

For the dead, they will be raised with a new imperishable body. For those who are alive, they will be "caught up" to meet the Lord in the air. As they are being caught up they will be changed, or transformed into a new body.

10. THEY WILL BE ANGEL-LIKE

The new bodies of believers will be angel-like. Jesus said.

For when the dead rise, they won't be married. They will be like the angels in heaven (Matthew 22:30 NLT).

While we will not become angels, our bodies will be similar to them in some respects.

Jesus spoke elsewhere about believers being like angels. Luke records Him saying the following about life in the next world.

But people who are considered worthy to come back to life and live in the next world will neither marry nor die anymore.

> They are the same as the angels. They are God's children who
> have come back to life (Luke 20:35,36 God's Word).

The idea seems to be that the new bodies do not have power to repro-
duce, or have any sexual drive. Jesus also said these new bodies of
believers will be deathless.

However, we must emphasize that we will not become angels. Angels
are a different order of being. In the Book of Genesis we are told that
God created everything "according to its kind."

Human beings have been created in the image of God. We are a different "kind" of being than the angels. The Bible says.

> Then God said, "Let us make man in our image, in our like-
> ness, and let them rule over the fish of the sea and the birds of
> the air, over the livestock, over all the earth, and over all the
> creatures that move along the ground" (Genesis 1:26 NIV).

We have been made in God's image, according to His likeness. We will
keep that divine image throughout all eternity. On the other hand,
Scripture never says that angels have been made in the image of God.
Thus, angel-like does not mean that we will actually become angels.

11. IT WILL BE A SPIRITUAL BODY

The new body will be "spiritual." The term "spiritual body" seems like
a contradiction of terms but it is not. Our present bodies are characterized by our soulish or fallen sinful nature. When our bodies are
changed, they will be characterized by the spirit, our new nature. While
it will still be a body it will be a different kind of body.

Paul emphasized this when he wrote.

> They are natural human bodies now, but when they are raised,
> they will be spiritual bodies. For just as there are natural bodies,
> so also there are spiritual bodies (1 Corinthians 15:42-44 NLT).

Although we will receive spiritual bodies, we will not be pure spirit. The emphasis is upon the new body in which we receive. Paul makes the comparison to our present sinful bodies which we now have to the new bodies we will receive, sinless or spiritual bodies.

Again, we stress the fact that this new body will be characterized by the spirit, therefore it will not be a sinful body!

12. THE BODY WILL BE IMMORTAL AND INCORRUPTIBLE

Our present bodies decay and die, our new bodies will not. There will be no decay, no disease and no death. Paul wrote.

> So also *is* the resurrection of the dead. *The body* is sown in corruption, it is raised in incorruption (1 Corinthians 15:42 NKJV).

These glorified bodies will not be subject to decay or corruption. They will not grow old nor will they deteriorate. Paul also wrote.

> This body that decays must be changed into a body that cannot decay. This mortal body must be changed into a body that will live forever (1 Corinthians 15:53 God's Word).

Immortality, in this context, means not subject to death, while mortal means perishable, or subject to death. The bodies of believers will not die. Indeed, they cannot die.

13. THE BODY WILL BE ADAPTABLE TO A NEW ENVIRONMENT

The new body will be from heaven, adaptable to the new environment. In other words, they will be heavenly bodies or bodies fit for the heavenly realm. Paul wrote.

> As was the man of dust, so also are those who are of the dust, and as is the man of heaven, so also are those who are of heaven. Just as we have borne the image of the man

of dust, we shall also bear the image of the man of heaven (1 Corinthians 15:48,49 ESV).

Our new bodies will be able to function both in heaven and on the new earth. This, of course, is in contrast to our present bodies which can only function here upon the earth.

Among other things, the glorified bodies of believers seems to call for a new earth on which we will live as well as in the new heaven. In fact, the doctrine of the resurrection of the body makes no sense whatsoever apart from the doctrine of the new earth on which we will also reside.

Scripture speaks of this creation of a new heavens and a new earth; a new universe.

> I saw a new heaven and a new earth, because the first heaven and earth had disappeared, and the sea was gone (Revelation 21:1 God's Word).

Consequently, our new bodies, like Jesus' body, will be able to function in the visible realm as well as the invisible realm. This is what the Scripture teaches.

However, it gives us few details as to exactly how this is possible. Like so many other things with respect to the afterlife, we must wait and see how all these wonderful promises will be fulfilled.

14. THE BODY WILL BE GLORIOUS

Scripture speaks of our new body as being glorious. Paul wrote of a future body that will be glorious. He said.

> It is sown in dishonor; it is raised in glory. It is sown in weakness; it is raised in power (1 Corinthians 15:43 ESV).

This is a powerful statement! Humans were made to live with God forever; not to be buried in the ground in dishonor and remain in the grave for all eternity. Therefore, our new body will be a body of "glory."

15. THE BODY WILL BE LUMINOUS: IT WILL SHINE

The new body will be luminous. Indeed, in the Book of Daniel we are told that the wise will shine like stars. The Bible says.

> And those who are wise shall shine like the brightness of the sky above; and those who turn many to righteousness, like the stars forever and ever (Daniel 12:3 ESV).

In a similar statement, Jesus said believers will shine as the sun.

> Then the godly will shine like the sun in their Father's Kingdom. Anyone who is willing to hear should listen and understand! (Matthew 13:43 NLT).

There will be something about the nature of the new body that will cause it to reflect the light of God or to shine.

A. MOSES FACE SHONE

We find examples of this in Scripture. The Bible says that Moses' face shone when he was in God's presence. In the Book of Exodus, we read the following.

> And the people would see his face aglow. Afterward he would put the veil on again until he returned to speak with the LORD (Exodus 34:35 NLT).

His encounter with the Lord caused his face to shine. This gives us a picture of our future bodies which will shine for the Lord.

B. JESUS' FACE SHONE LIKE THE SUN AT THE TRANSFIGURATION

At the Transfiguration, we are told that Jesus' face shone like the sun. Matthew recorded it as follows.

> And he was transfigured before them, and his face shone like the sun, and his clothes became white as light (Matthew 17:2 ESV).

The face of Jesus shone like the sun. In some sense, we will also shine with our new bodies.

C. ADAM AND EVE MAY HAVE BEEN CLOTHED WITH LIGHT

It is possible that Adam and Eve were clothed with some type of light garment before the Fall. After they fell, Adam and Eve realized that they had lost something.

We read in the Book of Genesis about their response.

> Then the eyes of both of them were opened, and they realized they were naked; so they sewed fig leaves together and made coverings for themselves (Genesis 3:7 NIV).

It has been supposed that they had lost some clothing of light when they sinned. This would explain why they immediately realized what they had done.

If they had some sort of garment of light in their perfected state, this would be consistent with the new bodies believers will receive; a bright or luminous body.

16. THE NEW BODY IS THE HOPE OF EVERY BELIEVER

Finally, we discover that the promised "new body" is the hope of every believer. Paul wrote to the Corinthians about the hope he had for a resurrection body. He emphasized that we have a building from God, a house, waiting for all of us who believe.

> We know that if the life we live here on earth is ever taken down like a tent, we still have a building from God. It is an eternal house in heaven that isn't made by human hands. In our present tent-like existence we sigh, since we long to put on the house we will have in heaven. After we have put it on, we won't be naked. While we are in this tent, we sigh. We feel distressed because we don't want to take off the tent,

but we do want to put on the eternal house. Then eternal life will put an end to our mortal existence. God has prepared us for this and has given us his Spirit to guarantee it (2 Corinthians 5:1-5 God's Word).

This passage contrasts our earthly house, our present body, with the eternal heavenly house that each believer will receive. This is the destiny of those who have believed in Jesus Christ!

CONCLUSION TO THE RESURRECTED BODIES OF THE RIGHTEOUS

These are some of the wonderful truths that the Bible teaches about the bodies which believers will receive. There is indeed a glorious future for those who have trusted the promises of the Lord; a glorified body.

SUMMARY TO QUESTION 9
WHAT WILL THE GLORIFIED BODIES OF THE RIGHTEOUS BE LIKE?

The Bible says that someday every believer in Jesus Christ will receive a new God-given body, a glorified body. Scripture gives us quite a bit of information about these future bodies of believers. This includes the following.

For one thing, the resurrected body of the believer will have a body like that of the resurrected Christ. This is the promise of Scripture. Consequently, we can learn much about our new bodies from an examination of what the Bible says about His.

This brings us to our next point. We will receive a literal body, an actual body. Jesus' resurrected body was real and so will ours be. Among other things, He could eat, drink and be touched. Since our body will be like His, we will be able to do the same things as He did.

While we will receive a new body, we will not have a new identity. Our real self will continue to exist. This means that we will be different from one another in the next life as we are here upon the earth.

We also learn that the new body will be related to our present body. In some sense, it will be the same body that was put in the grave, but in another sense it will be very different. What we do find from Scripture is that there will be some continuity between the old and the new. Though there will be a certain connection between the old and new, the nature of that connection is not explained. In other words, we will be in certain respects the same, while in other respects different.

This new body will also have new capacities. Just as the body of the resurrected Christ demonstrated abilities His earthly body did not possess our new body will have these same new capacities. It seems, therefore, we will be able to appear and disappear, move from one dimension to another, such as Christ did after His resurrection.

Scripture also says that our new bodies will be angel-like. We will not become angels because they are a different order of being. However our bodies will take on certain characteristics that angels presently have. Among other things, this means that we will not be subject to death.

In addition, we will find that this new body will be both permanent and indestructible. It will never grow old, decay or perish. It is deathless.

The glorified body is also called a spiritual body. We know that our present bodies are characterized by our own soulish or fallen nature. When our bodies are changed, they will then be characterized by the spirit, our new sinless nature. While it will still be a body it will be a different kind of body.

All in all, we must admit that there is some mystery with respect to the glorified body that the Scriptures do not fully explain. What we do know is that our new bodies will be something greater than anything we can imagine!

What Are Some Inadequate Views Of The Resurrection Of The Body?

The Bible provides us with information about the future bodies that believers will receive. These truths help us realize what the Lord has planned for those who have trusted Him.

However, there have been a number of inadequate views that have been put forward with respect to the resurrection of the body. These views do not accurately state what the Scripture has to say about our future bodies.

In other words, they are misconceptions of what the Bible actually says about the topic. Some of the main misconceptions can be stated as follows.

MISCONCEPTION 1: THERE IS NO RESURRECTION BODY

Some object to the idea of the bodily resurrection of believers because the New Testament never uses the phrase "resurrection of the body." Moreover, the Bible says the dead will receive a "spiritual body" as opposed to a natural body.

> It is sown a natural body; it is raised a spiritual body. If there is a natural body, there is also a spiritual body (1 Corinthians 15:44 ESV).

This, they argue, shows the Bible does not teach a bodily resurrection. Instead, believers will become spirits after their death.

RESPONSE

Though the exact phrase "resurrection body" is not found in the Scripture, the teaching certainly is. It is quite clear that believers will receive a new body at the resurrection; a body that is incorruptible. We can make the following observations.

OUR NEW BODY WILL BE CHARACTERIZED BY THE SPIRIT

The idea of the new body being a spiritual body, as opposed to a natural body, does not mean it has no physical form. It means the new body will be characterized by the new spiritual nature instead of the old sinful nature. The new nature is sinless, while the old nature could only sin. It is in this sense that believers will have a physical body which will also be a spiritual body.

MISCONCEPTION 2: WE WILL HAVE ANGELIC BODIES

It has been proposed that the bodies of believers will be the same nature as angels. Some have thought that this is the case from a statement from Jesus.

> The people of this age marry and are given in marriage. But those who are considered worthy of taking part in the age to come and in the resurrection from the dead will neither marry nor be given in marriage, and they can no longer die; for they are like the angels. They are God's children, since they are children of the resurrection (Luke 20:35,36 NIV).

It is claimed that Jesus taught that the bodies of believers will be like that of the angels. Upon death, believers will become members of the company of angels.

RESPONSE

The Bible never teaches that believers will become angels. Jesus was saying we will be "as" or "like" the angels in heaven. This means that we will be like them in at least two senses: we are deathless in the eternal state and there is no marrying or having children in heaven.

Angels do not die, neither do they marry or procreate. We will have those same characteristic in heaven. Indeed, there will be no marriages and no more additions to the human race.

We should also note that Jesus did not say that believers will have angel-like bodies. Angels are spirits who have no bodily form, at least no form such as ours. The writer to the Hebrews makes this clear.

> God said about the angels, "He makes his messengers winds. He makes his servants flames of fire . . . What are all the angels? They are spirits sent to serve those who are going to receive salvation (Hebrew 1:7,14 God's Word).

Believers will be clothed with a glorified body. Therefore, while in some sense we will be angel-like, in other senses we will be different.

MISCONCEPTION 3: IT WILL BE REANIMATION OF THE OLD BODY

It has been taught that the resurrection of believers is simply the reanimation of the old molecules such as what happened to Lazarus. The Bible says that he had been dead for four days when Jesus brought him back to life. In the same manner, as it was with Lazarus, it is our original body which will brought back to life.

RESPONSE

The Bible says that the coming resurrection is not the simple reanimation of the old molecules. The new body will be transformed with characteristics the old body did not have.

Indeed, these present bodies are subject to decay and death. Consequently, we need more than a mere re-animation of the old body. Our new bodies cannot grow old, nor can they die. This is the type of body we will need if we are going to live for all eternity.

MISCONCEPTION 4: IT WILL OCCUR BY NATURAL FORCES NOT BY A SUPERNATURAL ACT OF GOD

Could the resurrected body of the believer be merely the result of natural forces working on the body? Some people believe this is the case. Something, some unknown force, will put our bodies back together.

RESPONSE

The Bible is clear that the resurrection of the body will not be the result of natural forces working upon the body. It will be a supernatural work of God. In fact, Scripture emphasizes that the new bodies we will receive will be God-given. Indeed, this type of change could never happen naturally.

MISCONCEPTION 5: OUR NEW BODY WILL BE MOLECULE FOR MOLECULE THE SAME

The bodies of believers will be molecule for molecule the same body that was put in the grave. Though it will be a glorified body, it will be the exact same body that was buried.

RESPONSE

It will be the same body, in some sense, but the body will be a transformed, imperishable body. There is no need to insist it will be molecule for molecule the same. The Bible gives no indication that the body will be the same in every sense. While there will be continuity between the two there will also be differences.

MISCONCEPTION 6: IT WILL BE A FLESH AND BLOOD BODY

It has been thought that the body of the believer is a flesh and blood body, like the one we have now. The only difference is that it acquires some new powers.

RESPONSE

Flesh and blood speaks of our present human nature. The new body of believers will not be made up of the same flesh and blood like our present bodies. The Bible is specific about this.

Paul wrote to the Corinthians.

> What I am saying, dear brothers and sisters, is that flesh and blood cannot inherit the Kingdom of God. These perishable bodies of ours are not able to live forever (1 Corinthians 15:50 NLT).

The Bible also says the life of the creature is in the blood.

> For the life of any creature is in its blood. I have given you the blood so you can make atonement for your sins. It is the blood, representing life, that brings you atonement (Leviticus 17:11 NLT).

The new body we receive will seemingly have a different type of life source. The new body may be bloodless. There is no need for nourishment in the new bodies because the new bodies will never break down. The phrase, flesh and blood, speaks of these current bodies.

This sums up some of the misconceptions which people have about the resurrected bodies of believers. It is very important that these misunderstandings be cleared up so that we can have the correct view of what Scripture has to say about our promised glorified bodies.

SUMMARY TO QUESTION 10
WHAT ARE SOME INADEQUATE VIEWS OF THE RESURRECTION OF THE BODY?

It is crucial for us to realize that the Scripture alone is the only place where we can receive reliable information about the new bodies the Lord has promised us. Consequently, it is important that we discover what it teaches on this important issue.

In an attempt to understand the nature of the resurrected, or glorified bodies, of believers in Jesus Christ, there have been a number of inadequate theories or misconceptions which have been put forward. These misunderstandings need to be cleared up.

One false idea is that there is no resurrection body. Instead of a bodily resurrection some people argue for some type of spiritual resurrection where believers become spirits without bodies.

Yet the Scripture makes it clear that those who have believed in the Lord will receive a new body like that of the resurrected Christ. Indeed, our new body will be characterized by the spirit; it will be a spiritual body. It will be a sinless body as opposed to our present sinful body.

In addition, it will have new properties that our present bodies do not possess.

There is also the mistaken belief that the bodies of believers will actually become angels. While the Scripture says our new bodies will be angel-like, we will not become angels. Angels are a different order of being than humans. We will become angel-like in the sense that our new bodies will not be subject to decay or to death. Like the angels, we will be in a new form which will last for all eternity.

Some teach this body will now possess will simply be re-animated, not resurrected. In other words it will be the same old body brought back to life. This is clearly refuted by the example of Jesus. While others before Him were re-animated, they merely came back to life after they had died, He was the first to be resurrected. The others died again, Jesus did not! Our new bodies will not be able to die; contrary to the present bodies we possess.

There is also the teaching that natural forces, not supernatural forces, will raise our bodies back to life. Supposedly some unknown force will bring these bodies back to life. Scripture refutes this. It is the God of the Bible who makes alive these bodies which have died.

We also find the belief that the resurrected body of the believer will be molecule for molecule the same as the body that was put in the grave. While there is continuity between our present body and our new body, it will not be exactly the same. Indeed, our new bodies will be fit for eternity.

Finally, there are those who believe the resurrection body will be a flesh and blood body. Again, Scripture emphasizes that our new body will have properties our present body does not have.

In sum, none of these claims properly treats what the Bible has to say on the subject. Rather, they are misconceptions about the body we have been promised. The new body of the believer will be a glorified, resurrected body that is, in some sense, connected to the old body, but, in another sense, a brand new body.

While there is much that we do not know about these new bodies, Scripture has given us enough information so as to give us a basic understand of what lies ahead for each of us. It is indeed exciting!

What's The Difference Between Resurrection And Resuscitation Or Reanimation?

In Scripture, we have a number of examples of people who were dead and then brought back to life. Unfortunately, what happened to them is often confused with the doctrine of the resurrection of the dead. Were these people resurrected in the biblical sense or did something else happen to them? The key to understanding what took place is recognizing the difference between resurrection and re-animation or resuscitation.

Indeed, there is a huge difference between resurrection and resuscitation, or re-animation. Resurrection, in the biblical sense of the term, refers to putting on a new, glorified body, while re-animation, or resuscitation, means bringing the person back to life in the old, mortal body in which they died. Those who were resuscitated died again. Those who will be resurrected from the dead will never die again.

THE BIBLE LISTS A NUMBER OF RESUSCITATIONS

There are eight specific examples in Scripture where God resuscitated a person; He brought them back to life after they had died. They are as follows.

1. ELIJAH BROUGHT A CHILD BACK FROM DEATH

By the power of the Lord, Elijah brought back to life the son of a widow. We read of this episode in the Book of First Kings. It says the following.

> So the LORD listened to Elijah's voice, and the boy's life returned to him, and he lived (1 Kings 17:22 HCSB).

This was a miracle of resuscitation. The child was brought back to life. Yet it was not a resurrection in the biblical sense of the word. He would later die and remain dead.

2. ELISHA AND THE CHILD

Elisha the prophet also brought a child back from the dead. We read of this in the Book of Second Kings. The narrative reads as follows.

> When Elisha got to the house, he discovered the boy lying dead on his bed. So he went in, closed the door behind the two of them, and prayed to the LORD. Then he went up and lay on the boy: he put mouth to mouth, eye to eye, hand to hand. While he bent down over him, the boy's flesh became warm. Elisha got up, went into the house, and paced back and forth. Then he went up and bent down over him again. The boy sneezed seven times and opened his eyes (2 Kings 4:32-35 HCSB).

Here again, we find the Bible informing us about a resuscitation to life. Yet, this boy, like the rest of us, would eventually die, and this time, he would remain dead.

3. ELISHA'S BODY BROUGHT A DEAD PROPHET BACK TO LIFE

The Scripture says the body of the dead prophet Elisha was instrumental in bringing another prophet back from the dead.

> Then Elisha died and was buried. Now Moabite raiders used to come into the land in the spring of the year. Once, as the Israelites were burying a man, suddenly they saw a raiding party, so they threw the man into Elisha's tomb. When he touched Elisha's bones, the man revived and stood up (2 Kings 13:20,21 HCSB).

This was indeed a unique miracle. This resuscitation took place when the prophet came in contact with the bones of Elisha. Yet, like all of those who went before him, this unnamed prophet would eventually die again.

These Old Testament examples, of God reviving the dead, show us that He has the capability, as well as the desire, to restore life. The Lord said to Jeremiah.

> Behold, I *am* the LORD, the God of all flesh: is there any thing too hard for me? (Jeremiah 32:27 KJV).

However, as we have indicated, all those who were revived eventually died again. Their restoration is not the same thing as the promised resurrection of the dead.

NEW TESTAMENT EXAMPLES

As was true with Old Testament examples, the New Testament gives us the accounts of people who have been brought back from the dead.

4. LAZARUS WAS BROUGHT BACK TO LIFE

Lazarus had been dead for four days when the Lord Jesus brought Him back to life. The Bible explains what happened in this manner.

> So they took away the stone. And Jesus lifted up his eyes and said, "Father, I thank you that you have heard me. I knew that you always hear me, but I said this on account of the people standing around, that they may believe that you sent me." When he had said these things, he cried out with a loud voice, "Lazarus, come out." The man who had died came out, his hands and feet bound with linen strips, and his face wrapped with a cloth. Jesus said to them, "Unbind him, and let him go" (John 11:41-44 ESV).

Jesus raised His friend Lazarus back to life after he had been dead for four days. Yet, at some later time, Lazarus again died and then remained dead.

5. JAIRUS' DAUGHTER WAS RAISED BACK TO LIFE

The daughter of a man named Jairus was also raised from the dead by Jesus. Luke records it as follows.

> And all were weeping and mourning for her, but he said, Do not weep, for she is not dead but sleeping. And they laughed at him, knowing that she was dead. But taking her by the hand he called, saying, "Child, arise." And her spirit returned, and she got up at once. And he directed that something should be given her to eat (Luke 8:52-55 ESV).

The Bible tells us that this miracle astounded the people. However, this little girl, like everyone else, would eventually die again.

6. THE WIDOW OF NAIN'S SON WAS RAISED FROM THE DEAD

There was a woman in the city of Nain who had a son who had recently died. The Bible says that Jesus brought her son back from the dead.

> Then He came and touched the open coffin, and those who carried *him* stood still. And He said, "Young man, I say to you, arise." So he who was dead sat up and began to speak. And He presented him to his mother (Luke 7:14,15 NKJV).

Though he was brought back to life, this young man had to die again someday.

7. PETER BROUGHT DORCAS BACK TO LIFE

There was also a woman named Dorcas, or Tabitha, whom Peter raised from the dead. We read about this in the Book of Acts. It says.

> Then Peter sent them all out of the room. He knelt down, prayed, and turning toward the body said, "Tabitha, get up!" She opened her eyes, saw Peter, and sat up. He gave her his hand and helped her stand up. Then he called the saints and widows and presented her alive (Acts 9:40,41 HCSB).

This valuable woman was raised back to life so she could be of service to those in the early church. However, she too would one day die again.

8. PAUL RAISED EUTYCHUS

In the Book of Acts, we have the account of Paul bringing a young man named Eutychus back from the dead.

> And a young man named Eutychus, sitting at the window, sank into a deep sleep as Paul talked still longer. And being overcome by sleep, he fell down from the third story and was taken up dead. But Paul went down and bent over him, and taking him in his arms, said, "Do not be alarmed, for his life is in him." And when Paul had gone up and had broken bread and eaten, he conversed with them a long while, until daybreak, and so departed (Acts 20:9-11 ESV).

As is true with the other biblical examples, this young man eventually died and remained dead.

THESE RESUSCITATIONS WERE NOT PERMANENT

These are the biblical examples of people who were miraculously resuscitated or re-animated after they were dead. Each one of these examples is a miracle of the Lord.

However, this resuscitation was not something that lasted forever. Indeed, they were brought back to life in the same body that died. These people eventually experienced death for a second time.

In contrast, the promised glorified body for the believer is permanent. Indeed, it will never grow old or die.

Thus, we need to make the distinction between resuscitation and resurrection. They are not the same thing!

SUMMARY TO QUESTION 11
WHAT'S THE DIFFERENCE BETWEEN RESURRECTION AND RESUSCITATION OR REANIMATION?

Resurrection, according to Scripture, means bringing a person back to life in a brand new body. This resurrected, or glorified, body will never die. The promise of Scripture is that those who believe in the Lord Jesus will one day receive this body.

Resuscitation, on the other hand, refers to a person coming back to life in their present body. Those who are resuscitated or re-animated will eventually die for good.

The Bible gives several specific examples of people who were resuscitated, or re-animated. In other words, they came back to life after being dead.

We find three examples in the Old Testament. Resuscitations were attributed to the prophets Elijah and Elisha. In addition, we are told the bones of the dead prophet Elisha brought another prophet back to life.

In the gospels, there are three examples of resuscitations which are specifically attributed to Jesus. This includes the son of a widow from the city of Nain, the young daughter of a man named Jairus, and a friend of Jesus called Lazarus. These three had truly died and then were brought back to life by the Lord Jesus. However, each of them eventually died again.

The New Testament, in the Book of Acts, gives two other examples of people who were brought back to life in this manner. Peter brought back to life a woman named Dorcas. There is also the account of a young man named Eutychus who was resuscitated. Paul prayed over his dead body and he was brought back from the dead.

Each of these people who were brought back to life had to die again. Again we must emphasize that this is not the same as the biblical hope of resurrection.

When believers are raised from the dead, they will receive a new, glorified body. This new body will never perish. This is the difference between resurrection and resuscitation.

QUESTION 12

Isn't The Resurrection Of The Dead A Scientific Impossibility?

Some have thought that the idea of a bodily resurrection of the dead is not physically possible. Indeed, when people die the particles of their body enter into new combinations. Soon, nothing is left of that original body. In fact, our bodies turn into dust.

Furthermore many people have been cremated upon their death. There is nothing left of them but ashes. Others die in a fire or are eaten by animals. How, then, will their bodies be raised when there is nothing left of them?

There are a number of points that need to be made in answering these questions.

1. THERE IS NOT A MOLECULE FOR MOLECULE RESURRECTION

The Scripture does not teach a molecule for molecule resurrection. Paul wrote to the Corinthians about the nature of the resurrection. He stated it as follows.

> What you plant, whether it's wheat or something else, is only a seed. It doesn't have the form that the plant will have. God gives the plant the form he wants it to have. Each kind of seed grows into its own form. . . . That is how it will be when the dead come back to life. When the body is planted, it decays. When it comes back to life, it cannot decay (1 Corinthians 15:37-38,42 God's Word).

With the resurrected bodies of believers, there is a certain connection of the old and the new, but the exact nature of this connection is not revealed.

2. IT IS NOT IMPOSSIBLE FOR GOD

As to the possibility of the God of the Bible raising the dead, the following thoughts should be kept in mind. Jesus said.

> For with God nothing shall be impossible (Luke 1:37 KJV).

Nothing is impossible for the God of Scripture. Nothing!

Paul said to a pagan ruler that a resurrection from the dead is not too difficult for the God of the Bible. He put it this way.

> Why should any of you consider it incredible that God raises the dead? (Acts 26:8 NIV).

Again, nothing is impossible for the God of Scripture. He has the power to do such a miraculous deed.

In fact, the Lord Himself is quoted as saying.

> I am the LORD, the God of all mankind. Is anything too hard for me? (Jeremiah 32:27 NIV).

He can do whatever He wishes. There is nothing which is too difficult for Him.

3. GOD ORIGINALLY CREATED SOMETHING FROM NOTHING

There is something else which must be kept in mind. When God created the universe He made something out of nothing. The writer to the Hebrews put it this way.

> By faith we understand that the universe was created by the word of God, so that what is seen was not made out of things that are visible (Hebrews 11:3 ESV).

Since God created the universe out of nothing, it certainly would not be a problem for Him to make a resurrection body out of something! If we can accept the statement that God spoke the entire universe into existence, then the idea of Him raising the bodies of the dead does not seem so incredible.

4. HE HAS NOT TOLD US HOW HE IS GOING TO DO IT

While we know that God is going to change our mortal bodies into bodies that are immortal, He has not explained the process.

Indeed, the Bible merely says that God will change our corruptible body into something incorruptible. In other words, He has not told us how He is going to accomplish it. Therefore, any speculation as to how He will do it is fruitless. However, rest assured, He can and will do it!

ONE SUGGESTION: HE HAS OUR TEARS IN A BOTTLE

While we do not know exactly how the Lord will resurrect our mortal bodies I would like to share a suggestion that a young man once gave to me. After speaking on the subject, and mentioning the fact that we do not know how the Lord is going to change our dead bodies into glorified bodies, this man asked me a question. He said, "Doesn't the Bible say that the Lord collects all our tears in a bottle?"

It indeed does. We read in Psalms.

> You keep track of all my sorrows. You have collected all my tears in your bottle. You have recorded each one in your book (Psalm 56:8 NLT).

He then said, "Well, if He has collected all our tears, then He has our DNA!" Indeed!

Whatever the case may be, we know that someday, somehow, the God of the Bible will transform our mortal and corruptible bodies into bodies that immortal and incorruptible.

SUMMARY TO QUESTION 12
ISN'T THE RESURRECTION OF THE DEAD A SCIENTIFIC IMPOSSIBILITY?

There are those who believe that the resurrection of the body is a physical impossibility. They contend that it is not possible for the dead to come back to life. Our bodies will eventually turn to dust. In addition, what about those who are cremated or are eaten by animals? It seems impossible to sort out the molecules of these deceased people.

Yet the Scriptures make it very clear that the living God will someday raise our dead bodies back to life. Several things should be noted about this.

First, the new bodies are not molecule for molecule the same. The new body will have some similarities, but will not exactly be the same as our present body. Therefore, He does not have to collect every molecule from our body to make a new, glorified body for us.

Second, the resurrection of the body is not something impossible for God. The God of Scripture is powerful enough to do this. In fact, nothing is too difficult for Him.

Indeed, in the beginning, God created something out of nothing when He made the universe. He spoke and the universe came into existence. If He is able to do that, He is certainly able to change our bodies from mortal to immortal.

As to how He will do it, we simply do not know because He has not told us. Yet we know it is certainly not beyond His power.

Does The Bible Teach That Both The Righteous And Unrighteous Will Be Raised From The Dead?

Scripture speaks of two distinct resurrections; that of the just and that of the unjust. All Bible believers agree that there will be a resurrection of both the believing and unbelieving dead. The Word of God has the following things to say about this matter.

THERE IS A RESURRECTION OF THE RIGHTEOUS

The resurrection of the righteous is described in Scripture in the following ways.

1. THE AWAKENING TO EVERLASTING LIFE

Some of the dead, those who sleep in the dust, will awake to everlasting life. The prophet Daniel wrote.

> Multitudes who sleep in the dust of the earth will awake: some to everlasting life . . . (Daniel 12:2 NIV).

The bodies of the dead, while presently sleeping in the graves, will be awakened someday. This is one way in which the resurrection is described.

2. THE RESURRECTION OF THE RIGHTEOUS

The Bible also says the believers will be raised at the "resurrection of the righteous." Jesus spoke of this time. He said.

> But when you give a banquet, invite the poor, the crippled, the lame, the blind, and you will be blessed. Although they cannot repay you, you will be repaid at the resurrection of the righteous (Luke 14:13,14 NIV).

There will be a resurrection of those who are righteous, those who have placed their faith in the God of Scripture.

3. THE RESURRECTION OF LIFE

Jesus also spoke of the resurrection "of life" or a resurrection "which leads to life." We read of this in John's gospel. It says.

> Do not be amazed at this, because a time is coming when all who are in the graves will hear His voice and come out— those who have done good things, to the resurrection of life . . . (John 5:28,29 HCSB).

There is a resurrection of the dead which will lead to eternal life.

4. THE BETTER RESURRECTION

The writer to the Hebrews wrote of a better resurrection. He put it this way.

> Women received back their dead, raised to life again. There were others who were tortured, refusing to be released so that they might gain an even better resurrection (Hebrews 11:35 NIV).

Those who believe in the Lord can look forward to this "better resurrection."

5. THE FIRST RESURRECTION

The Apostle John said that after the Second Coming of Christ there will be a first resurrection. We read of this in the Book of Revelation.

It says.

> Then I saw thrones, and people seated on them who were
> given authority to judge. I also saw the people who had
> been beheaded because of their testimony about Jesus and
> because of God's word, who had not worshiped the beast
> or his image, and who had not accepted the mark on their
> foreheads or their hands. They came to life and reigned with
> the Messiah for 1,000 years . . . This is the first resurrection
> (Revelation 20:1-5 HCSB).

Only the righteous will take part in the first resurrection.

THE RESURRECTION OF THE UNRIGHTEOUS

The resurrection of the unrighteous is also described in Scripture by a
number of different terms. This can be observed as follows.

1. THE AWAKENING TO SHAME AND EVERLASTING CONTEMPT

Daniel spoke of a resurrection of disgrace for those who do not believe
in the Lord. He described it like this.

> Multitudes who sleep in the dust of the earth will awake:
> some to . . . shame and everlasting contempt (Daniel 12:2
> NIV).

Those who do not believe will have their own resurrection but it will be
one of disgrace. This shame and contempt will be everlasting.

2. THE RESURRECTION OF CONDEMNATION

Jesus also spoke of a resurrection of condemnation, or a resurrection
which would lead to judgment or condemnation. We read of this in
the Gospel of John.

> Do not be amazed at this, because a time is coming when all
> who are in the graves will hear His voice and come out . . .

those who have done wicked things, to the resurrection of judgment (John 5:28,29 HCSB).

The Contemporary English Version puts it this way.

> Don't be surprised! The time will come when all of the dead will hear the voice of the Son of Man, and they will come out of their graves. . . . everyone who has done evil things will rise and be condemned (John 5:28,29 CEV).

Condemnation, or judgment, is what this resurrection will bring to those who have not believed.

3. THE RESURRECTION OF THE UNRIGHTEOUS

The Bible speaks of the resurrection of the unrighteous. The Book of Acts records Paul the Apostle saying the following.

> And I have a hope in God, which these men themselves also accept, that there is going to be a resurrection, both of the righteous and the unrighteous (Acts 24:15 HCSB).

The unrighteous will be raised.

Therefore, from God's Word we find that there will be a resurrection of the dead which will include both the righteous and the unrighteous. The descriptive terms used of each of them makes it clear as to the fate of those who are brought back to life. Indeed, it will be fabulous blessings or horrific judgment!

SUMMARY TO QUESTION 13
DOES THE BIBLE TEACH THAT BOTH THE RIGHTEOUS AND UNRIGHTEOUS WILL BE RAISED FROM THE DEAD?

The Scripture makes it plain that there will come a time when everyone who has ever lived will be raised from the dead. There will be a resurrection of the righteous as well as the unrighteous.

In other words, everyone will be raised for the purpose of a judgment on their lives. There is no escaping this judgment.

The resurrection of the righteous is compared to awakening those who have slept. The bodies of the believers, asleep in the graves, will be awakened to everlasting life. This resurrection is also called the resurrection of the righteous, the resurrection of life, the better resurrection, and the first resurrection. The judgment for the believer will not be one of condemnation, but rather the giving of rewards.

In contrast to this, the resurrection of the lost is known as the awakening to disgrace and contempt. Jesus referred to it as the resurrection of condemnation, or the resurrection which leads to condemnation. We also find it termed the resurrection of the unrighteous.

It is clear from these descriptions that these two resurrections could not be more different. One leads to life while the other leads to death. One leads to rewards while the other leads to judgment.

Hopefully, everyone who is reading this is on their way to the resurrection that leads to life.

What About The Unbelievers? How Will They Be Raised? Will They Have A Body?

We have seen that not only the righteous will be raised from the dead, the Bible says that the wicked will be raised also. If so, then what does it say about them when they are raised?

Scripture provides us with some information about what will happen to the unrighteous in the next world. The following points need to be made about the raising of the wicked.

1. UNBELIEVERS WILL RISE FROM THE DEAD

To begin with, the Bible is clear regarding the resurrection of unbelievers. The Apostle Paul said that both the righteous and unrighteous will someday be raised from the dead.

We find him making the follow statements about the future resurrection which will include the unrighteous. He said.

> I admit that I worship the God of our ancestors as a follower of the Way, which they call a sect. I believe everything that is in accordance with the Law and that is written in the Prophets, and I have the same hope in God as these men themselves have, that there will be a resurrection of both the righteous and the wicked (Acts 24:14,15 NIV).

Paul cited the prophets as predicting the same things which he was proclaiming. They taught, as did he, that there was going to come a day when the dead will be raised. This includes everyone, the righteous as well as the ungodly. Thus, unbelievers will be raised.

Jesus also said that the righteous as well as the unrighteous will be raised at some time in the future. John records Him saying the following.

> Do not marvel at this; for the hour is coming in which all who are in the graves will hear His voice and come forth — those who have done good, to the resurrection of life, and those who have done evil, to the resurrection of condemnation (John 5:28-29 NKJV).

There will be a resurrection of unbelievers. Contrary to the resurrection of the believers, the resurrection of unbelievers is called the resurrection of condemnation.

2. IT HAS NOT HAPPENED YET

This resurrection is still yet future. Indeed, the resurrection of the wicked dead has not yet occurred in a single case.

The Apostle Paul made this clear in his letter to Timothy. We find that some people were teaching that the resurrection of the dead had already occurred. He made it plain that the resurrection of those who have died is an event which is still to come. In fact, he said that those who taught that the resurrection had already occurred were preaching a lie.

> They have left the path of truth, preaching the lie that the resurrection of the dead has already occurred; and they have undermined the faith of some (2 Timothy 2:18 NLT).

Therefore, it was an error to say the resurrection had already taken place in the past. Indeed, it is yet future.

What Paul wrote to Timothy still holds true today. There will be a resurrection of the dead in the future and this will include the unrighteous.

3. THERE IS NO EXPLANATION OF THEIR BODY

We now consider an interesting fact with respect to the bodies of the wicked dead. While the Scripture gives much detail with respect to the bodies of the saved, there is absolutely nothing said in the Bible with respect to the bodies of the lost. We know they are raised and judged. Yet Scripture is silent as to what form they will assume upon their resurrection. Not one thing is explicitly said about what sort of body, or form, they will have.

4. THIS IS A CONSISTENT BIBLICAL PATTERN

This silence is in keeping with the totality of Scripture. Those who have died without trusting Jesus Christ are never named in Scripture. Likewise, the Bible nowhere described the bodies of unbelievers. The purpose for their resurrection is one of judgment and punishment. Only the basic facts are given.

This is a consistent pattern of Scripture. The ungodly dead are not described in detail or highlighted. Only those who belong to the Lord and will enter His kingdom are the ones which are important. The others will be condemned.

A. NO AGES ARE GIVEN OF THE UNGODLY

We find another example of this in the Book of Genesis. In Genesis chapters four and five, the godly and ungodly are listed in a genealogy. However, there is no age given of those in the ungodly line. Only the godly have their age listed. Again, the stress is only the godly ones. The ungodly are treated as they never really existed.

B. THE UNGODLY RICH MAN IS NOT NAMED

The ungodly rich man, in Jesus' story in Luke 16, likewise remains nameless. While the righteous Lazarus, the poor beggar, is named the ungodly man is not. This is further indication of who the Lord takes notice of. It is His children, not the unrighteous.

Therefore, the fact that the final form of the ungodly is not explained is to be expected. What we find emphasized in Scripture is God and His relationship with His children. Those who have rejected Him are not the main concern of the Bible. Consequently, their names, as well as their form, are not a subject that is given any explanation.

SUMMARY TO QUESTION 14
WHAT ABOUT THE UNBELIEVERS? HOW WILL THEY BE RAISED? WILL THEY HAVE A BODY?

The Bible teaches that there will be a resurrection of the wicked as well as a resurrection of the righteous. This is plainly taught in Scripture.

Indeed, Jesus spoke of a time when the graves would be opened and the wicked and righteous would be raised. Upon hearing His voice, the dead would be raised.

The Apostle Paul said the same thing; there will be a resurrection of the dead. Furthermore, he stressed the fact that there would come a time when the unbelievers would be raised.

This raising of the wicked dead has not happened yet. At the time of Paul there were those who were claiming that the resurrection was a thing of the past. It is not. The raising of the righteous dead and the unrighteous dead remains something which will happen in the future.

As to what form the unrighteous will assume upon their resurrection, the Bible does not say. Therefore, it is useless to speculate as to how they will look for all eternity. However, we do know that they will be raised in some type of form. Beyond this, we cannot say anything for certain.

The reason more is not said about the unrighteous is simple; unbelievers are not the main characters in the biblical narrative. In fact, they are not usually named at all. For example, in Jesus' story of the rich man and Lazarus the unrighteous rich man is unnamed. Though he had status in this life it is though he did not exist in the next.

Therefore, we are only told as much about the unrighteous as is necessary to the central story of Scripture. Since they have rejected God's free gift of salvation in this life they will be condemned in the next as a nameless soul. What sort of physical form they will have, from which they will suffer God's punishment, is not revealed to us.

What Are The Biblical Arguments That Everyone Be Raised From The Dead At The Same Time? (One General Resurrection)

Though all Bible believers acknowledge that both the righteous and unrighteous dead will eventually be raised from the dead, there is no agreement as to the time when it will occur.

There are those who believe that everyone, both the righteous and the unrighteous, will be resurrected at the same time. However, others believe the different resurrections are spaced out over a period of time.

THE CASE FOR ONE GENERAL RESURRECTION

Many people believe the Bible teaches that the resurrection of the dead will take place at one particular time. The arguments for this can be listed as follows.

1. DANIEL WROTE THAT ALL THE DEAD ARE RAISED TOGETHER

The Lord told the prophet Daniel that the righteous and unrighteous will be raised together at the time of the end. We read the following in the Book of Daniel.

> At that time shall arise Michael, the great prince who has charge of your people. And there shall be a time of trouble, such as never has been since there was a nation till that time. But at that time your people shall be delivered, everyone

whose name shall be found written in the book. And many of those who sleep in the dust of the earth shall awake, some to everlasting life, and some to shame and everlasting contempt (Daniel 12:1-2 ESV).

This seems to be speaking of one resurrection for the righteous and the unrighteous which will take place at the same time. Indeed, it appears to be clear that there is no time lag between them.

2. JESUS SAID THERE WOULD BE A DAY OF RESURRECTION

When Jesus spoke of a future resurrection He seems to say the righteous and unrighteous will be judged at the same time. John records Him saying.

Don't be so surprised! Indeed, the time is coming when all the dead in their graves will hear the voice of God's Son, and they will rise again. Those who have done good will rise to eternal life, and those who have continued in evil will rise to judgment (John 5:28,29 NLT).

This also seems to be clear. There is a particular judgment "day." On that day, some will be given eternal life while others will suffer eternal punishment or everlasting retribution.

3. EVERYONE WILL BE RAISED ON THE LAST DAY

In another place, Jesus indicated the resurrection would occur on the "last day." Again, this seems to necessitate that believers and unbelievers being raised and judged at the same time.

We also read about this in the gospel of John. It says.

This is the will of Him who sent Me: that I should lose none of those He has given Me but should raise them up on the last day. For this is the will of My Father: that everyone who sees the Son and believes in Him may have eternal life, and

I will raise him up on the last day . . . Jesus answered them, "Stop complaining among yourselves. No one can come to Me unless the Father who sent Me draws him, and I will raise him up on the last day . . . Anyone who eats My flesh and drinks My blood has eternal life, and I will raise him up on the last day (John 6:39,40,44,54 HCSB).

Once again, we find that the resurrection of the dead, for both the righteous and unrighteous, will occur on the "last day." This does not seem to allow any time between resurrections.

4. MARTHA OF BETHANY BELIEVED IN A GENERAL RESURRECTION

We find that Martha, the sister of Lazarus, believed there would be a general resurrection of the dead at the "last day." We read the following dialogue between her and Jesus.

"Your brother will rise again," Jesus told her. Martha said, "I know that he will rise again in the resurrection at the last day" (John 11:23,24 HCSB).

Jesus did not correct her idea of the timing of the resurrection of the dead. This seems to give further evidence of this event occurring at one particular time, the last day.

5. PAUL SPOKE OF A DAY OF JUDGMENT

We also find that the Apostle Paul spoke of a "day" when God would judge the world. In the city of Athens, he said the following to a crowd which had gathered.

Therefore, having overlooked the times of ignorance, God now commands all people everywhere to repent, because He has set a day on which He is going to judge the world in righteousness by the Man He has appointed. He has provided proof of this to everyone by raising Him from the dead (Acts 17:30,31 HCSB).

Paul says that God has set a "day" in which He will judge the world. This is a further indication that the resurrection will occur on one particular day because resurrection always comes before judgment.

In another place, the apostle spoke of everyone being raised together. We read his words as recorded in the Book of Acts.

> And I have a hope in God, which these men themselves also accept, that there is going to be a resurrection, both of the righteous and the unrighteous (Acts 24:15 HCSB).

He does not mention any interval of time between the resurrection of the righteous and that of the unrighteous. Seemingly these resurrections occur simultaneously.

The Apostle Paul also wrote that Jesus Christ would judge those when He appeared. Again, judgment cannot occur without a resurrection. He put it this way in his second letter to Timothy.

> I charge you therefore before God and the Lord Jesus Christ, who will judge the living and the dead at His appearing and His kingdom (2 Timothy 4:1 NKJV).

Again we find that the living and the dead will be judged when Jesus returns.

To many people, these passages clearly speak of one general resurrection of both the saved and lost.

6. THE GREAT WHITE THRONE JUDGMENT IS A ONE TIME EVENT

There is something else. The Bible speaks of that day when everyone is judged. This is known as the "Great White Throne Judgment." The Scripture says that the Lord appears on a huge throne and passes judgment on every human being who has ever lived. Before these people are judged they are all raised from the dead.

John, the writer of the Book of Revelation, put the matter in the following way.

> The Devil who deceived them was thrown into the lake of fire and sulfur where the beast and the false prophet are, and they will be tormented day and night forever and ever. Then I saw a great white throne and One seated on it. Earth and heaven fled from His presence, and no place was found for them. I also saw the dead, the great and the small, standing before the throne, and books were opened. Another book was opened, which is the book of life, and the dead were judged according to their works by what was written in the books. Then the sea gave up its dead, and Death and Hades gave up their dead; all were judged according to their works. Death and Hades were thrown into the lake of fire. This is the second death, the lake of fire. And anyone not found written in the book of life was thrown into the lake of fire (Revelation 20:10-15 HCSB).

Here we find that the dead are raised and judged. In this passage, there is no time distinction between the resurrections recorded in this passage. Death and Hades gives up its dead as well as the sea giving up the dead in it. Therefore, it seems that all those who have died, from the beginning of the human race, are now raised together at this one moment in time.

Thus, it is argued that from the totality of Scripture, that there seems to be one day in the future where everyone, who has ever lived, is raised from the dead.

While the character of the resurrection will not be the same for everyone, with some going to glory and others going to damnation, there will be only one resurrection day. This, it is argued, is what the Bible teaches about the coming resurrection of the dead.

SUMMARY TO QUESTION 15
WHAT ARE THE BIBLICAL ARGUMENTS THAT EVERYONE BE RAISED FROM THE DEAD AT THE SAME TIME? (ONE GENERAL RESURRECTION)

The Bible says that everyone who has ever died will eventually be raised from the dead. All Bible-believers agree upon this. However, they do not agree as to the timing of the resurrection of the dead.

There are many who think the Bible teaches that there will be one general resurrection where everyone is raised at the same time. The reasons for holding this perspective can be given as follows.

In the Old Testament, the prophet Daniel spoke of a time when the dead are raised, both unrighteous and righteous. No time interval is mentioned between these resurrections.

In the New Testament, Jesus spoke of a "day" or "time" when the dead hear His voice and are raised for the purpose of judgment. Again, no interval is spoken of between the time of the resurrection of the saved and of the lost.

In another place, Jesus spoke of raising up the believer on the "last day." This is further indication that there is a general resurrection of the dead and that it will occur on one particular day.

Martha, the sister of the dead man Lazarus spoke of a "day" when the dead are raised. She said it would be on the "last day." She did this in the presence of Jesus and He did not correct her. There was no idea of an interval of time between the resurrection of the righteous and unrighteous.

Finally, the Apostle Paul wrote of a future time when the Lord will judge the living and the dead. He told the people in Athens that it would happen on a "day" which God has set. This is a further indication that the resurrection of the dead occurs at one particular time.

The Bible describes this last judgment in the Book of Revelation. The Lord sits on a Great White Throne and judges all of the dead. This judgment covers each and every person who has ever lived. Indeed, this passage says that the sea will give up their dead as well as death and hades giving up the dead in them. This seems to be a comprehensive resurrection of everyone who has ever lived and died.

These passages have convinced many that the resurrection of the dead will be a one-time event. There is no idea of multiple resurrections in the Scripture.

What Are The Biblical Arguments That There Is More Than One Resurrection?

While there are many good Bible-believing Christians who think the Scripture teaches that everyone will be raised on the same day, there are others who believe that the resurrection from the dead, along with the accompanying judgments, will not all occur at the same time. In other words, the resurrection from the dead will not happen on one particular day but rather over a period of time. A couple of points need to be made.

THE LAST DAY DOES NOT MEAN ONE LITERAL DAY

To begin with, those whose reject one general resurrection for everyone do not think the passages which are cited prove that all will be raised at once. In fact, all that these passages are saying is there will be a resurrection of the righteous and unrighteous at the "last hour" or "last day."

This, it is argued, is an undetermined period of time and could stretch over a thousand years. Indeed, the Greek word translated "day" can have the meaning of an indeterminate amount of time. In fact, the standard Greek Lexicon has the following entry under the Greek word for day.

> An extended period like the Hebrew word *yom* (A Greek Lexicon Of The New Testament, Bauer, Danker, Arndt and Gingrich).

Since this is certainly a possible meaning of the term, many think it is better to understand the Bible as teaching that a number of separate resurrections will occur. The arguments are as follows.

THERE WILL BE SEPARATE RESURRECTIONS FOR BELIEVERS AND UNBELIEVERS

There are a number of passages that seem to call for a separate resurrection of believers from the unbelievers. For example, we find the Bible speaking of a "first" resurrection. John wrote.

> Then I saw thrones, and people seated on them who were given authority to judge. I also saw the souls of those who had been beheaded because of their testimony about Jesus and because of God's word, who had not worshiped the beast or his image, and who had not accepted the mark on their foreheads or their hands. They came to life and reigned with the Messiah for 1,000 years. The rest of the dead did not come to life until the 1,000 years were completed. This is the first resurrection. Blessed and holy is the one who shares in the first resurrection! The second death has no power over these, but they will be priests of God and the Messiah, and they will reign with Him for 1,000 years (Revelation 20:4-6 HCSB).

In this passage, we have the souls of the believing dead waiting for their own resurrection. This takes place after the Second Coming of Jesus Christ to the earth.

IT IS CALLED THE FIRST RESURRECTION

When they are raised it is called the "first resurrection." The fact that there is a first resurrection certainly implies a second resurrection. Furthermore, those who participate in the "first resurrection" are called blessed. In fact, those who do not experience this first resurrection will experience the "second death."

THERE IS A SECOND RESURRECTION ONE THOUSAND YEARS LATER

Indeed, we are told that the rest of the dead will not be raised for another thousand years. This is the Great White Throne Judgment which is then described in this manner.

> Then I saw a great white throne and One seated on it. Earth and heaven fled from His presence, and no place was found for them. I also saw the dead, the great and the small, standing before the throne, and books were opened. Another book was opened, which is the book of life, and the dead were judged according to their works by what was written in the books. Then the sea gave up its dead, and Death and Hades gave up their dead; all were judged according to their works. Death and Hades were thrown into the lake of fire. This is the second death, the lake of fire. And anyone not found written in the book of life was thrown into the lake of fire (Revelation 20:11-15 HCSB).

These people are raised one thousand years later for the purpose of judgment. These are the people who will experience the "second death."

If these thousand years are literal years, and the two resurrections described are each literal resurrections, then this seems to make two separate resurrections absolutely necessary. Consequently, it is not possible that everyone can be raised and judged at once.

PAUL SPOKE OF HIS DESIRE TO BE RAISED

The Apostle Paul made a statement about his own resurrection that seems to confirm this. It reads as follows.

> My goal is to know Him and the power of His resurrection and the fellowship of His sufferings, being conformed to His death, assuming that I will somehow reach the resurrection from among the dead (Philippians 3:10,11 HCSB).

Note that Paul is looking forward to be raised "from among the dead." If all were to be raised together, then why would he make such a statement? His words seems to assume a separate resurrection of the believers from the unbelievers. He wants to be raised "out from among the dead" with the other believers. This assumes that not everyone will be raised at that time.

This is consistent with what Jesus said about the resurrection of the dead.

> The people of this age marry and are given in marriage. But those who are considered worthy of taking part in the age to come and in the resurrection from the dead will neither marry nor be given in marriage, and they can no longer die; for they are like the angels. They are God's children, since they are children of the resurrection (Luke 20:34-36 NIV).

Jesus spoke of those "who are worthy" will take part in the coming age and the resurrection from the dead. While this is obviously a distinct group from those who are lost, His words also may indicate that this resurrection takes place before the resurrection of the unbelievers. The fact that they are called "children of the resurrection" may also indicate that we are looking at a resurrection which takes place before the resurrection of the unbelievers.

To sum up, His words are consistent with the idea of distinct resurrections; one that takes place for the saved and then later another one that is for the lost.

THE VARIOUS RESURRECTIONS OCCUR IN A PARTICULAR ORDER

As we examine the totality of Scripture we find that there are a number of resurrections which take place in a particular order.

Jesus Christ's resurrection was first in God's program, then to be followed by believers. Paul wrote about this to the Corinthians.

For just as in Adam all die, so also in Christ all will be made alive. But each in his own order: Christ, the firstfruits; afterward, at His coming, the people of Christ (1 Corinthians 15:22,23 HCSB).

When Paul says each in his own order, it has the idea of a marching unit of the Roman army. The picture is of a great triumphal procession in which a general returns victorious from a battle while the troops march behind him in different ranks.

The resurrection of the dead will be similar. Jesus Christ will be the first, followed by a number of groups who come back from the dead, each in their own marching order.

THE ORDER OF THE RESURRECTIONS

The Bible, therefore, seems to speak of two future resurrections, the resurrection of life and the resurrection of death. The first resurrection is in four parts or phases. The various resurrections that the Bible speaks about are as follows.

1. The Resurrection Of Jesus Christ

2. The Saved At Rapture Of The Church

3. The Tribulation Saints And Old Testament Saints At His Second Coming

4. The Great White Throne And Millennial Saints

We can cite the evidence as follows.

1. JESUS CHRIST IS THE FIRST TO BE RAISED

Jesus Christ was the first person to come back from the dead, never to die again. Paul wrote about this to the Corinthians.

But now Christ has been raised from the dead, the first-fruits of those who have fallen asleep. For since death came

> through a man, the resurrection of the dead also comes through a man. For as in Adam all die, so also in Christ all will be made alive. But each in his own order: Christ, the firstfruits; afterward, at His coming, those who belong to Christ (1 Corinthians 15:20-23 HCSB).

He is called the firstfruits of those who have died. Others will come after.

In the Book of Acts, as Paul was preaching the message of Jesus, he made the following statement about the resurrection of Christ.

> To this very day, I have obtained help that comes from God, and I stand and testify to both small and great, saying nothing else than what the prophets and Moses said would take place — that the Messiah must suffer, and that as the first to rise from the dead, He would proclaim light to our people and to the Gentiles (Acts 26:22-23 HCSB).

Jesus the Messiah was the first to rise from the dead; never to die again.

When Paul wrote to the Colossians, he spoke of Christ's pre-eminence in everything. He used the illustration that Christ was the first to come back from the dead.

> He is also the head of the church, which is his body. He is the beginning, the first to come back to life so that he would have first place in everything (Colossians 1:18 God's Word).

He is the One who is pre-eminent over death by being the first person who came back from the dead and then remained alive.

2. THE RAPTURE OF THE CHURCH

At the rapture of the church, the bodies of the living and dead will be changed from mortal to immortal. Paul wrote the following to the Thessalonians.

> For the Lord Himself will descend from heaven with a shout,
> with the archangel's voice, and with the trumpet of God,
> and the dead in Christ will rise first (1 Thessalonians 4:16
> HCSB).

The dead rise first, then the living believers will be caught up to meet the Lord in the air.

Paul told the church at Corinth about the change that would take place at this time. He explained it in this manner.

> Behold, I tell you a mystery: We shall not all sleep, but we shall
> all be changed—in a moment, in the twinkling of an eye, at
> the last trumpet. For the trumpet will sound, and the dead will
> be raised incorruptible, and we shall be changed. For this cor-
> ruptible must put on incorruption, and this mortal *must* put
> on immortality. So when this corruptible has put on incor-
> ruption, and this mortal has put on immortality, then shall be
> brought to pass the saying that is written: "Death is swallowed
> up in victory." "O Death, where *is* your sting? O Hades, where
> *is* your victory?" The sting of death *is* sin, and the strength of
> sin *is* the law. But thanks *be* to God, who gives us the victory
> through our Lord Jesus Christ. Therefore, my beloved breth-
> ren, be steadfast, immovable, always abounding in the work of
> the Lord, knowing that your labor is not in vain in the Lord
> (1 Corinthians 15:51-58 NKJV).

Those Christians who are alive at this time will be "raptured" or "caught up" to meet the Lord in the air. As they are being caught up, their bodies will be changed.

This event happens only to believers. Indeed, there is no such thing as a "catching up" and then "changing" the bodies of those who have not believed. Consequently, there is no resurrection of the lost at this time.

3. THE TRIBULATION SAINTS

There are still others to be raised. The tribulation saints, those who become believers in Jesus Christ during the Great Tribulation period, will be raised at the Second Coming of Christ.

In the Book of Revelation, we read the following.

> I saw thrones on which were seated those who had been given authority to judge. And I saw the souls of those who had been beheaded because of their testimony about Jesus and because of the word of God. They had not worshiped the beast or his image and had not received his mark on their foreheads or their hands. They came to life and reigned with Christ a thousand years. (The rest of the dead did not come to life until the thousand years were ended.) This is the first resurrection. Blessed and holy are those who have part in the first resurrection. The second death has no power over them, but they will be priests of God and of Christ and will reign with him for a thousand years (Revelation 20:4-6 NIV).

These saints will be raised when the Lord Jesus returns to the earth at His Second Coming. This will happen after the church saints, the body of Christ, have been either raptured or resurrected.

4. THE OLD TESTAMENT SAINTS

The believers, who lived before the time of Christ, will be raised when Jesus Christ returns. The Book of Daniel says.

> Michael, the chief of the angels, is the protector of your people, and he will come at a time of terrible suffering, the worst in all of history. And your people who have their names written in The Book will be protected. Many of those who lie dead in the ground will rise from death. Some of them will be given eternal life, and others will receive nothing but eternal shame and disgrace (Daniel 12:1-2 CEV).

After the tribulation period is over, Jesus Christ returns. He will then resurrect the Old Testament saints.

Consequently, every believer who has died, from the time of Adam until the Second Coming of Christ, will have been resurrected by this time.

THE INTERVAL: THE THOUSAND YEARS OF PEACE

When Christ returns, there will be a thousand year period of peace when He rules the world in righteousness. This is known as the Millennium. During this time, people will be born, live and die. However, it seems that no resurrections will occur during this period.

5. THE GREAT WHITE THRONE JUDGMENT

At the end of the thousand years, there will be a final resurrection. This will come at the Great White Throne judgment. The Book of Revelation writes of this event. It says.

> Then the Devil, who betrayed them, was thrown into the lake of fire that burns with sulfur, joining the beast and the false prophet. There they will be tormented day and night forever and ever. And I saw a great white throne, and I saw the one who was sitting on it. The earth and sky fled from his presence, but they found no place to hide. I saw the dead, both great and small, standing before God's throne. And the books were opened, including the Book of Life. And the dead were judged according to the things written in the books, according to what they had done. The sea gave up the dead in it, and death and the grave gave up the dead in them. They were all judged according to their deeds. And death and the grave were thrown into the lake of fire. This is the second death—the lake of fire. And anyone whose name was not found recorded in the Book of Life was thrown into the lake of fire (Revelation 20:10-15 NLT).

The resurrection of unbelievers will take place after the thousand year reign of Christ upon the earth. All the unbelieving dead who have ever lived will be resurrected and judged at this time.

SOME OF THE RIGHTEOUS ARE RAISED AT THIS TIME ALSO

Seemingly, there will also be some righteous people who will be raised at the Great White Throne judgment. They will consist of people who entered the Millennium as well as children who were born during this time and became believers in Jesus. These children will have been born to people who entered the Millennium with mortal, non-resurrected bodies. We assume that some of them will have died during this thousand year period. These people who have trusted Jesus will not be condemned but rather they will be rewarded at this time.

Though Scripture does not give us any specifics about when they are raised, or in the case of those still living, transformed into a glorified body, we assume at happens either at the Great White Throne judgment or at some unnamed time close to the "final judgment."

We can infer this because after the Great White Throne judgment we are told the following.

> I saw a new heaven and a new earth, because the first heaven
> and earth had disappeared, and the sea was gone (Revelation
> 21:1 God's Word).

Since the new heaven and new earth appear right after this last judgment, the remaining believers will have had to have been rewarded, as well as having their bodies changed, so they can enter the eternal realm. Therefore, it appears that the final judgment will consist of both rewards and condemnation.

In sum, from looking at the totality of Scripture, it seems necessary that the resurrection of the dead will take place over a period of time.

SUMMARY TO QUESTION 16
WHAT ARE THE BIBLICAL ARGUMENTS THAT THERE IS MORE THAN ONE RESURRECTION?

Although some Christians believe there will be only one general resurrection at the end of time, it is argued that Scripture seems to speak of more than one resurrection. The evidence can be listed as follows.

The first resurrection will be that of believers while the second resurrection will be that of unbelievers. These resurrections in Scripture do not all happen at once.

The first resurrection refers to the resurrection of all believers, though separated in time. The first Person to come back from the dead was Jesus Christ.

There has been over nineteen hundred and fifty years between the resurrection of Christ, and the rapture of the church; which is still future. There will be a resurrection of the dead associated with the time when the living believers are caught up to meet the Lord in the air.

After the church is raptured and the New Testament believers resurrected, there will be the resurrection of the tribulation saints. This will occur at the Second Coming of Christ to the world. These are people who have died for their testimony of Jesus Christ during the Great Tribulation period. At that time, the Old Testament saints will also be raised.

After the thousand-year reign of Christ on the earth, the Millennium, there will be one final resurrection. This will consist of the unrighteous dead from all time as well as the millennial saints; those who believed in Christ during the Great Tribulation period and entered the Millennium as well as those who were born to these people and trusted the Lord during this one thousand year period. After the Great White Throne judgment, there will be no more resurrections.

This sums up the position of those who believe there will not be one general resurrection of the dead but rather separate resurrections.

Since We Are Going To Get A New Body, How Should We View Our Present Sinful Body? Should We Hate It?

The wonderful promise of Scripture is that someday believers will have a new body. This body will be immortal; it will never grow old, decay, or die.

Paul wrote to the Corinthians about this fantastic truth. He said.

> I'm telling you a mystery. Not all of us will die, but we will all be changed. It will happen in an instant, in a split second at the sound of the last trumpet. Indeed, that trumpet will sound, and then the dead will come back to life. They will be changed so that they can live forever. This body that decays must be changed into a body that cannot decay. This mortal body must be changed into a body that will live forever. When this body that decays is changed into a body that cannot decay, and this mortal body is changed into a body that will live forever, then the teaching of Scripture will come true: "Death is turned into victory! Death, where is your victory? Death, where is your sting?" (1 Corinthians 15:51-55 God's Word).

In light of these truths, how should we treat our present body? Should we despise it? Should we treat it with contempt because a new body awaits us? What does the Bible say?

1. GOD PERSONALLY FORMED THE BODIES OF ADAM AND EVE

The Bible says that our bodies are special. In fact, the Book of Genesis says that God Himself formed the body of Adam, the first human, from the dust of the ground.

> Then the LORD God formed the man from the dust of the earth and blew the breath of life into his nostrils. The man became a living being (Genesis 2:7 God's Word).

God then formed the first woman, Eve, from the body of the man. The Bible explains what happened in this manner.

> The LORD God said, "It is not good for the man to be alone. I will make a helper suitable for him." So the LORD God caused the man to fall into a deep sleep; and while he was sleeping, he took one of the man's ribs and closed up the place with flesh (Genesis 2:18,21 NIV).

Therefore, our bodies were fashioned in the way which God wanted them to be. Indeed, they are not a mistake of evolution or a product of blind chance. They are special and we must treat them as such.

2. WE MUST REALIZE WE HAVE INFINITE WORTH

Although this is only a temporary body which we are now living in, we have infinite worth. Jesus Christ died for us as we are today; not for whom we shall become. The Bible says.

> Look at it this way: At the right time, while we were still helpless, Christ died for ungodly people. Finding someone who would die for a godly person is rare. Maybe someone would have the courage to die for a good person. Christ died for us while we were still sinners. This demonstrates God's love for us (Romans 5:6-8 God's Word).

As sinners, we are still of infinite worth to the Lord. This includes our current sinful bodies. These are the bodies for which Christ died.

Peter explained it this way.

> For you know that God paid a ransom to save you from the empty life you inherited from your ancestors. And the ransom he paid was not mere gold or silver. It was the precious blood of Christ, the sinless, spotless Lamb of God (1 Peter 1:18,19 NLT).

Therefore, we should treat our bodes with respect, not despise them.

3. WE SHOULD BE THANKFUL FOR OUR PRESENT BODY

Consequently each of us should be thankful for our present body. While we realize we are going to be receiving something better, we also know that this body we now possess has been designed by God. Indeed, the Apostle Paul said we should give thanks for all things.

He wrote to the Thessalonians.

> No matter what happens, always be thankful, for this is God's will for you who belong to Christ Jesus (1 Thessalonians 5:18 NLT).

One of the things, for which we should be thankful, are the bodies that God has given to us.

4. WE TREAT OUR BODIES PROPERLY

Our bodies are called the temple of the Holy Spirit. Paul wrote the following to the Corinthians explaining this important truth.

> Don't you know that your body is a temple that belongs to the Holy Spirit? The Holy Spirit, whom you received from God, lives in you. You don't belong to yourselves You were bought for a price. So bring glory to God in the way you use your body (1 Corinthians 6:19,20 God's Word).

Because our bodies are a temple of the Holy Spirit we should treat them properly. Indeed, we should not abuse them.

5. WE NEED TO REALIZE WHAT OUR BODIES CAN AND CANNOT DO

There is something else we should put into practice. God made us for a purpose. Our bodies were designed by Him to serve that purpose. Therefore, there are certain things we will be able to do while there are other things we cannot do. We should realize our various strengths, as well as our limitations. These bodies were not made to last forever.

6. WE SHOULD NOT COMPARE OUR BODY TO OTHERS

All of these things should teach us not to compare our bodies to others or wish that we looked differently. While we may look at our body and wish it had parts like that of another person; a flatter stomach, more attractive nose, better skin, etc., we should be thankful for what we are; not what we are not!

In fact, one of the Ten Commandments says that we should not covet or desire something that our neighbor has. It says.

> Do not covet your neighbor's house. Do not covet your neighbor's wife, male or female servant, ox or donkey, or anything else your neighbor owns (Exodus 20:17 NLT).

Therefore, we should not covet or desire what other people have. This includes how they look.

7. WE SHOULD LOOK FORWARD TO THE DAY WHEN WE RECEIVE OUR NEW BODY

Finally, we should look forward to that time when we receive a new body. No matter how well we treat this present body it is decaying and will eventually cease to exist. Paul emphasized this to Timothy.

> For physical training is of some value, but godliness has value
> for all things, holding promise for both the present life and
> the life to come (1 Timothy 4:8 NIV).

Scripture recognizes that physical training, or exercise, is of some value. However, the aging process and the deteriorating of our bodies is inevitable. Therefore, we must recognize these facts and look forward to the day when we will have a new body that will never grow old or deteriorate.

In sum, we should treat our present body in a proper manner as we await the time when we will receive a new body.

SUMMARY TO QUESTION 17
SINCE WE ARE GOING TO GET A NEW BODY, HOW SHOULD WE VIEW OUR PRESENT SINFUL BODY? SHOULD WE HATE IT?

The Bible promises that one day, we who believe in Jesus Christ, will receive a new body. Until that time we have to live in these fallen sinful bodies. What should be our attitude toward them?

First, we should appreciate that our bodies were directly formed by God Himself. He created Adam from the dust of the ground and Eve was made from the body of Adam. This fact makes it clear that our bodies are special seeing they were designed by God.

Furthermore, these bodies have infinite worth. Indeed, Jesus Christ has died for us while we are in these sinful bodies. This is a further reason not to hate the body which we have.

In addition, the Bible says we are to be thankful for all things. This includes the body we now have. Indeed, the fact we are even alive is something we should be thankful for.

These truths should cause us to give thanks for our present body. Consequently, we should treat our bodies properly. The Bible says that our body is the temple of the Holy Spirit since He dwells inside each of us.

Moreover, we should not compare ourselves to others. The Bible says that we should not covet or desire what other people have. This includes their looks. God made each of us as individuals and we should thank Him for His workmanship.

THE COMING BIBLICAL JUDGMENTS
How God Will Judge the Human Race

We have seen that death is not the end of our existence. The day will come when the Living God will resurrect the dead. But this leads to the next phase; the Biblical judgments.

The topic of this section of the book are these biblical judgments. Whom God will judge? When will these judgments occur? On what basis will people be judged?

This section will cover these and other crucial questions about the various judgments of God.

QUESTION 18

Will The Human Race Be Judged In The Future?

People do not like to think of God as a Judge. We would rather think of Him as our friend, our helper, and the One who deeply loves us. While all of these descriptions do describe the character of the God of the Bible, they do not give us the entire picture. God is also a judge. Indeed, the Bible has much to say about the topic of God's judgment of the human race.

WHERE JUDGMENT FITS INTO GOD'S OVERALL PLAN FOR HUMANITY

Before we look at what the Bible has to say about the various judgments which are to come, we must first understand where this doctrine of judgment fits into the overall plan and purpose of God.

After we pass on from this life, all of us go to an intermediate, or an in-between state. In this state we are conscious. Believers are with the Lord while unbelievers are separated from Him. This intermediate state is only temporary. There will come a day when the Lord will raise the dead, both the righteous and the unrighteous. The resurrection of the dead is for the purpose of judgment. Thus, there will come a day when all humanity is judged.

Now that we a basic understanding of where judgment fits in the overall plan of God, we want to look extensively at what the Bible has to say about this important subject.

1. GOD HAS JUDGED HUMANITY IN THE PAST

The Bible makes it clear that the living God has already judged the human race in the past. Indeed, He often appears in the Old Testament as the Judge of all the earth.

In fact, Abraham said the following to the Lord.

> Far be it from you to do such a thing—to kill the righteous with the wicked, treating the righteous and the wicked alike. Far be it from you! Will not the Judge of all the earth do right? (Genesis 18:25 NIV).

To Abraham, the Lord was the Judge of the entire earth.

The God of the Bible is also known as the God of justice. The prophet Malachi described Him in this manner.

> You have wearied the LORD with your words. "How have we wearied him?" you ask. By saying, "All who do evil are good in the eyes of the LORD, and he is pleased with them" or "Where is the God of justice?" (Malachi 2:17 NIV).

God is a just God, a fair and righteous God.

In the New Testament, Peter reminded his readers of God's judgment. He put it this way.

> And God did not spare the ancient world—except for Noah and his family of seven. Noah warned the world of God's righteous judgment. Then God destroyed the whole world of ungodly people with a vast flood (2 Peter 2:5 NLT).

God judged the ancient world. Many other examples can be found in Scripture when God has judged both individuals and nations. There is no doubt that God has exercised His judgment of the human race in the past.

2. GOD IS PRESENTLY JUDGING PEOPLE

Not only has God judged those in the past, the Bible says that He is presently judging people. Paul wrote to Corinthians about the judgment or discipline which God is currently practicing.

> If we were properly evaluating ourselves, we would not be judged, but when we are judged, we are disciplined by the Lord, so that we may not be condemned with the world (1 Corinthians 11:31-32 HCSB).

Past and present judgment is not what is under consideration here. We want to look at God's judgment of humanity with respect to the future life. Is there really going to be a final judgment of the human race? Does the Bible teach an ultimate judgment of humanity?

3. THE OLD TESTAMENT SPOKE OF FUTURE JUDGMENT

In the Old Testament, we find a number of passages dealing with the future judgment of the human race. Isaiah the prophet wrote of this day.

> Look, the LORD will come with fire His chariots are like the whirlwind to execute His anger with fury, and His rebuke with flames of fire. For the LORD will execute judgment on all flesh with His fiery sword, and many will be slain by the LORD (Isaiah 66:15,16 HCSB).

The Lord will execute His righteous judgment on all humanity. Of this, there is no doubt.

The prophet Ezekiel recorded the Lord predicting a time when the nations would be judged by the Him. The Lord Himself spoke of this judgment. We read.

> I will display My glory among the nations, and all the nations will see the judgment I have executed and the hand I have laid on them (Ezekiel 39:21 HCSB).

There will come a day when the Lord will judge the nations.

The prophet Joel also recorded the Lord speaking of a future judgment of the nations. He said.

> For behold, in those days and at that time, when I restore the fortunes of Judah and Jerusalem, I will gather all the nations and bring them down to the Valley of Jehoshaphat. And I will enter into judgment with them there, on behalf of my people and my heritage Israel, because they have scattered them among the nations and have divided up my land (Joel 3:1-2 ESV).

This is an awesome description of the future judgment which is going to occur.

We also find the prophet Zephaniah writing of a judgment of the assembled nations.

> "Therefore wait for me," declares the LORD, "for the day when I rise up to seize the prey. For my decision is to gather nations, to assemble kingdoms, to pour out upon them my indignation, all my burning anger; for in the fire of my jealousy all the earth shall be consumed" (Zephaniah 3:8 ESV).

Therefore, the Old Testament speaks of a judgment which will take place in the future.

4. THE NEW TESTAMENT SPEAKS OF A FUTURE JUDGMENT

While the Old Testament spoke of a future judgment of humanity, the idea is more fully developed in the New Testament. Indeed, the future judgment of the human race is a major theme in the New Testament. There is much evidence of this coming judgment.

JESUS SPOKE OF JUDGMENT

The idea of a future judgment is found in the teachings of the Lord Jesus. We learn a number of things from what His teachings. They include the following.

A. THERE WOULD BE A JUDGMENT DAY

He spoke of a time of judgment for the people who lived in His day. Matthew records Him saying the following.

> I assure you, Tyre and Sidon will be better off on the judgment day than you! (Matthew 11:22 NLT).

From this we learn that there will be a judgment day for humanity. We also find that those who rejected Him, when they witnessed His miracles, would receive harsher judgment than certain evil cities in the past.

B. JESUS WILL JUDGE EVERY HUMAN BEING

In another place, Jesus spoke of a final judgment for all humanity. John records the following words of Jesus to the religious leaders of His day.

> And he has given him authority to judge because he is the Son of Man. Do not be amazed at this, for a time is coming when all who are in their graves will hear his voice and come out—those who have done what is good will rise to live, and those who have done what is evil will rise to be condemned. By myself I can do nothing; I judge only as I hear, and my judgment is just, for I seek not to please myself but him who sent me (John 5:27-30 NIV).

Every human being is to be judged by Him.

C. JESUS WILL JUDGE THE NATIONS

Jesus also spoke of a future judgment of the nations. We read of this in Matthew where our Lord said the following.

The Son of Man will come in all his glory. All the angels will come with him. Then he will sit on his throne in the glory of heaven. All the nations will be gathered in front of him. He will separate the people into two groups. He will be like a shepherd who separates the sheep from the goats. He will put the sheep to his right and the goats to his left (Matthew 25:31-33 NIV).

Undoubtedly, Jesus taught there is going to be a future judgment of all humanity. He believed each human being would be judged by the living God.

PAUL SPOKE OF JUDGMENT

A recurring theme in the ministry of the Apostle Paul is that God will judge humanity at some time in the future. In the city of Athens, he said.

He has set a day when he will judge the world's people with fairness. And he has chosen the man Jesus to do the judging for him. God has given proof of this to all of us by raising Jesus from death (Acts 17:31 CEV).

God has appointed a special time of judgment.

When Paul spoke to the ruler Felix about the essentials of the Christian faith, he assured this ruler there would be a judgment to come. We read the following in the Book of Acts.

After some days Felix came with his wife Drusilla, who was Jewish, and he sent for Paul and heard him speak about faith in Christ Jesus. And as he reasoned about righteousness and self-control and the coming judgment, Felix was alarmed and said, "Go away for the present. When I get an opportunity I will summon you (Acts 24:24,25 ESV).

We find the coming judgment was part of Paul's discussion about the basic teachings of the Christian faith. Felix, like many people, did not want to hear of any such thing.

In the letters of Paul, the fact of the coming judgment is unmistakable. He wrote to the Romans about this.

> Do you really think God won't punish you, when you behave exactly like the people you accuse? (Romans 2:3 CEV).

Paul also wrote to the Romans about God's wrath toward the unbeliever which He will demonstrate on judgment day. He said the following.

> Since you are stubborn and don't want to change the way you think and act, you are adding to the anger that God will have against you on that day when God vents his anger. At that time God will reveal that his decisions are fair (Romans 2:5 God's Word).

We learn that God will vent His holy anger toward unbelievers on judgment day. We also discover that all the decisions He will make will be fair.

The Apostle Paul emphasized the judgment would be through the person of Jesus Christ. He also said to the Romans.

> Some people naturally obey the Law's commands, even though they don't have the Law. This proves that the conscience is like a law written in the human heart. And it will show whether we are forgiven or condemned, when God has Jesus Christ judge everyone's secret thoughts, just as my message says (Romans 2:16 CEV).

Clearly, the Apostle Paul taught that God was going to judge humanity in the future. There is no doubt about this.

PETER SPOKE OF THE COMING JUDGMENT

We also find the Apostle Peter talking about God's future judgment. In the Book of Acts we find him giving the following testimony to the Gentile Cornelius.

> And he ordered us to preach everywhere and to testify that Jesus is the one appointed by God to be the judge of all—the living and the dead (Acts 10:42 NLT).

Note that Jesus will be the Judge of the living as well as the dead.

In his letters, Peter wrote about judgment day. We read the following in First Peter about this coming judgment.

> They will give account to him who is ready to judge the living and the dead (1 Peter 4:5 ESV).

Peter also wrote about judgment in his second letter to the believers. He put it this way.

> Then the Lord knows how to deliver the godly out of temptations and to reserve the unjust under punishment for the day of judgment (2 Peter 2:9 NKJV).

Peter taught that judgment day was coming. Indeed, he emphasized that the Lord would deliver the godly but judge the ungodly.

JAMES SPOKE OF A FUTURE JUDGMENT

The writer James gives allusions to future judgments. He said the following.

> Talk and act as people who are going to be judged by laws that bring freedom. No mercy will be shown to those who show no mercy to others. Mercy triumphs over judgment (James 2:12,13 God's Word).

He too, spoke of a future judgment day.

JUDE WROTE OF GOD'S COMING JUDGMENT

Jude also speaks of God's judgment on humanity. He cited past judgments of the Lord as well as the promise of a future judgment. He wrote.

> You also know about the angels who didn't do their work and left their proper places. God chained them with everlasting chains and is now keeping them in dark pits until the great day of judgment. . . . Enoch was the seventh person after Adam, and he was talking about these people when he said: Look! The Lord is coming with thousands and thousands of holy angels to judge everyone. He will punish all those ungodly people for all the evil things they have done. The Lord will surely punish those ungodly sinners for every evil thing they have ever said about him (Jude 6,14,15 CEV).

This is another indication of God's judgment on the human race.

THE BOOK OF HEBREWS SPEAKS OF A COMING JUDGMENT

The writer to the Hebrews also teaches the fact of God will someday judge the entire human race. He put it this way.

> And just as it is appointed for people to die once—and after this, judgment —so also the Messiah, having been offered once to bear the sins of many, will appear a second time, not to bear sin, but to bring salvation to those who are waiting for Him (Hebrews 9:27,28 HCSB).

Judgment is going to happen to every human being. The writer to the Hebrews also claimed that judgment was a basic doctrine of the faith.

> Therefore let us leave the elementary teachings about Christ and go on to maturity, not laying again the foundation of repentance from acts that lead to death, and of faith in God, instruction about baptisms, the laying on of hands, the resurrection of the dead, and eternal judgment (Hebrews 6:1-2 NIV).

According to this passage, eternal judgment is an elementary doctrine of the Christian faith. Judgment is a certainty

JOHN WROTE OF THE FUTURE JUDGMENT

The beloved disciple, John, also taught the future judgment of God. In his first letter, we read these words from him.

> Children, stay one in your hearts with Christ. Then when he returns, we will have confidence and won't have to hide in shame (1 John 2:28 CEV).

Since judgment day is coming, believers should to act in such a way in which they will not be put to shame.

THE BOOK OF REVELATION SPEAKS OF A COMING JUDGMENT

In many places in the Book of Revelation we find John speaking of the coming judgment. For example, we find these references.

> That terrible day has come! God and the Lamb will show their anger, and who can face it? (Revelation 6:17 CEV).

No one can stop God's judgment of humanity.

A. BELIEVERS WILL BE REWARDED AND UNBELIEVERS PUNISHED

The judgment will consist of rewards for believers and condemnation for unbelievers. We read of this in the Book of Revelation. It says.

> When the nations got angry, you became angry too! Now the time has come for the dead to be judged. It is time for you to reward your servants the prophets and all of your people who honor your name, no matter who they are. It is time to destroy everyone who has destroyed the earth (Revelation 11:18 CEV).

He will reward the faithful and condemn the unfaithful.

B. THERE WILL BE A FINAL JUDGMENT FOR HUMANITY

There will be a final judgment when humanity will be gathered before the Lord. John wrote of this awesome event.

> I saw a great white throne with someone sitting on it. Earth and heaven tried to run away, but there was no place for them to go. I also saw all the dead people standing in front of that throne. Every one of them was there, no matter who they had once been. Several books were opened, and then the book of life was opened. The dead were judged by what those books said they had done (Revelation 20:11,12 CEV).

This is a breathtaking description of what will happen in the future.

THIS JUDGMENT INVOLVES REMEMBERING THE THINGS WE HAVE DONE

God's judgment will involve remembering things done on the earth. The Bible says that the sins of Babylon will be remembered by the Lord.

> Her sins are piled as high as heaven, and God has remembered her crimes (Revelation 18:5 God's Word).

God will judge those sins.

Those whose names are not written in the Book of Life will be judged. They will receive the punishment of the Lord.

> And all the people who belong to this world worshiped the beast. They are the ones whose names were not written in the Book of Life before the world was made—the Book that belongs to the Lamb who was slaughtered (Revelation 13:8 NLT).

Jesus had earlier spoken of a judgment day where everything will be remembered. Matthew records Him saying the following.

> I can guarantee that on judgment day people will have to give an account of every careless word they say. By your words you will be declared innocent, or by your words you will be declared guilty (Matthew 12:36,37 God's Word).

The Bible says that God will remember every deed that has been done. Jesus emphasized this in a parable that Matthew records. He said the following to those who were going to be condemned.

> Then they too will answer, 'Lord, when did we see You hungry, or thirsty, or a stranger, or without clothes, or sick, or in prison, and not help You?' (Matthew 25:44 HCSB).

God takes note of everything that we do; even if we do not remember it.

FINAL JUDGMENT IS DENIED BY UNBELIEVERS

While the Bible clearly speaks of a final judgment for all humanity, unbelievers deny this truth. The Bible recognizes their denial. Paul wrote.

> There is no fear of God before their eyes (Romans 3:18 KJV).

The New Living Translation says.

> They have no fear of God to restrain them (Romans 3:18 NLT).

In fact, they live as though there will not be any judgment. Yet, Peter says their judgment is certain. He wrote of this coming judgment.

> First, you must understand this: In the last days people who follow their own desires will appear. These disrespectful people will ridicule God's promise by saying, "What's happened to his promise to return? Ever since our ancestors died, everything continues as it did from the beginning of the world (2 Peter 3:3-4 God's Word).

While the thought of a judgment is a comfort for believers it also serves as a warning for unbelievers.

Therefore, from the beginning of Scripture until the end, the fact of God's judgment of humanity is clearly taught. The Lord, the righteous Judge, will cause every human being to come before Him in judgment. Judgment is indeed coming!

SUMMARY TO QUESTION 18
WILL THE HUMAN RACE BE JUDGED IN THE FUTURE?

Though many people do not like to think of God as a judge, the Bible describes Him as the righteous judge. The doctrine of God's judgment fits into His overall plan and purpose for the human race.

After we die, each of us remains in a conscious state apart from our human body. The righteous are with the Lord while the unrighteous are apart from Him. However, this is only an intermediate or in-between state. There will come a time when the dead are raised and the bodies and spirits are re-united. This resurrection is for the purpose of judgment. Thus, God will judge the human race in the future.

From the pages of Scripture we discover that God has judged humanity in the past. The Bible records God judging individuals as well as nations. Furthermore, Scripture says that He is presently judging the human race.

As God has judged humanity in the past with both rewards and condemnation, He will also judge the same way in the future. Both testaments speak of a final judgment of God.

Indeed, the judgment of the human race is a major theme in Scripture. In fact, the Apostle Paul, as well as the writer to the Hebrews, taught that eternal judgment was one of the foundational beliefs of the Christian faith.

Everyone will be judged for what they have done here upon earth. There will be no exceptions. We will all have to give an account for our lives.

Scripture teaches a day of judgment. It will be a definite event. It will not be an endless process. Judgment will involve God remembering all the deeds that humans have done. Everything we do will be evaluated.

While unbelievers deny God's judgment will occur, the Bible emphasizes that God's judgment is certain. Indeed, it will happen someday.

Therefore, all of us can look forward to a day when we will be judged by God.

Who Will Be The Judge Of Humanity? What Does The Bible Have To Say About Jesus Judging The World?

The fact that humanity will be judged is clear. There will come a day when all of us must give an account of our life. The Scripture also makes it clear that the God of the Bible will be the judge.

Furthermore, we learn that Jesus Christ, God the Son, will be that judge of all humanity. The Bible says the following about the God's judgment of the human race.

1. THE LORD WILL BE THE JUDGE

Scripture says that the Lord, the God of the Bible, will judge the human race. The psalmist wrote about this as follows.

> Yet, the Lord is enthroned forever. He has set up his throne for judgment. He alone judges the world with righteousness. He judges its people fairly (Psalm 9:7,8 God's Word).

The Lord will judge the world and He will judge it righteously and in fairness.

The Apostle Paul also acknowledged that God would judge humanity. He wrote of this in his letter to the Romans.

They are fully aware of God's death penalty for those who do these things, yet they go right ahead and do them anyway. And, worse yet, they encourage others to do them, too (Romans 1:32 NLT).

The God of the Bible will be the judge of the human race. Paul also said that people are aware that God will indeed judge them. However, they continue to rebel against Him even though they know that judgment is coming.

2. GOD THE SON, JESUS CHRIST, WILL JUDGE

It is also clear that God the Son will be the judge. We find this from Jesus' own statement, the writings of Paul, the words of Peter, as well as the testimony of the Book of Revelation.

A. JESUS' STATEMENT THAT HE WILL JUDGE

Jesus made it plain that all judgment has been entrusted to Him. The Gospel of John records Jesus saying.

> The Father doesn't judge anyone, but he has made his Son the judge of everyone (John 5:22 CEV).

Jesus will be the Judge.

Jesus said all the nations will be judged by Him when He returns to the earth a second time. Matthew records Jesus' teaching.

> When the Son of Man comes in his glory and all his angels are with him, he will sit on his glorious throne. The people of every nation will be gathered in front of him. He will separate them as a shepherd separates the sheep from the goats. He will put the sheep on his right but the goats on his left (Matthew 25:31-33 God's Word).

Jesus Himself will separate the believers from the unbelievers.

B. THE APOSTLE PAUL TAUGHT THAT JESUS WOULD BE THE FINAL JUDGE

He wrote the following to Timothy.

> I solemnly urge you in the presence of God and Christ Jesus, who will someday judge the living and the dead when he appears to set up his Kingdom (2 Timothy 4:1 NLT).

According to Paul, Jesus will be our Judge.

C. THE TESTIMONY OF THE APOSTLE PETER ABOUT JESUS' JUDGMENT

Peter also emphasized that judgment will come through God the Son. In the Book of Acts, we read of Peter's words to a group of Gentiles who were inquiring about the faith. He put it this way.

> He ordered us to warn the people, 'God has appointed Jesus to judge the living and the dead' (Acts 10:42 God's Word).

Jesus will judge the human race at some future time.

D. THE BOOK OF REVELATION SAYS JESUS WILL BE THE JUDGE

Finally, we discover that the nations of the world will be judged by Jesus at His return. The Book of Revelation records Jesus saying that everyone will be judged.

> Look, I am coming soon, bringing my reward with me to repay all people according to their deeds (Revelation 22:12 NLT).

Jesus testifies that He will judge the world upon His return.

3. WHAT WE LEARN OF THE JUDGMENT OF JESUS

From an examination of Scripture, we learn the following things about the judgment of Jesus Christ that is still to come.

A. JESUS WILL JUDGE RIGHTEOUSLY

Jesus will judge righteously. In fact, He Himself testified to this fact.

> I can do nothing on My own. I judge only as I hear, and My judgment is righteous, because I do not seek My own will, but the will of Him who sent Me (John 5:30 HCSB).

His judgment will be righteous, it will be fair.

We also read of this in the Book of Acts. Paul said to a crowd in the city of Athens about Jesus' ability to righteously judge.

> He has set a day when he will judge the world's people with fairness. And he has chosen the man Jesus to do the judging for him. God has given proof of this to all of us by raising Jesus from death (Acts 17:31 CEV).

Jesus will judge everyone with fairness.

The writer to the Hebrews also emphasized this truth. He wrote about the righteousness of God the Son. We read the following in the first chapter of Hebrews.

> But of the Son he says, "Your throne, O God, is forever and ever, the scepter of uprightness is the scepter of your kingdom. You have loved righteousness and hated wickedness (Hebrews 1:8,9 ESV).

Jesus Christ, God the Son, will be the righteous judge.

B. HE WILL JUDGE OUR HEARTS

God the Son will judge the secrets of our hearts. Paul wrote the following to the Romans about this fact. He said.

> The day will surely come when God, by Jesus Christ, will judge everyone's secret life. This is my message (Romans 2:16 NLT).

The hearts of everyone will be judged by God the Son, Jesus Christ. Indeed, He knows what is in our heart.

C. JUDGMENT OCCURS WHEN HE COMES AGAIN

Judgment will occur at His Second Coming. In the last part of his final letter, Paul emphasized this to Timothy when he wrote these words.

> I solemnly call on you in the presence of God and Christ Jesus, who is going to judge those who are living and those who are dead. I do this because Christ Jesus will come to rule the world (2 Timothy 4:1 God's Word).

When Jesus appears a second time, people will be judged.

D. JESUS WILL JUDGE BELIEVERS AND UNBELIEVERS DIFFERENTLY

While all people will be judged by Jesus, not everyone will be judged the same. Those who have believed in Him will suffer no punishment or condemnation. Paul wrote.

> So those who are believers in Christ Jesus can no longer be condemned (Romans 8:1 God's Word).

However, those who have not believed in Him are presently in a state of condemnation. John recorded the following.

> Whoever believes in him is not condemned, but whoever does not believe stands condemned already because he has not believed in the name of God's one and only Son (John 3:18 NIV).

Therefore, Jesus will reward the believers and punish the unbelievers when He judges humanity at some time in the future.

E. HE HAS THE AUTHORITY TO JUDGE

Jesus Christ has the qualifications to be the judge of humanity, because He is the living God who became a human being. We read about this in John's gospel. It says.

> And he has given him authority to judge all mankind because
> he is the Son of Man (John 5:27 NLT).

Jesus has the ability, as well as the authority, to judge.

F. HE KNEW WHAT WAS IN HUMANS

Jesus is in a position to judge us because He knows what is inside of humans. We find the following description of this in the Gospel of John.

> But Jesus knew what was in their hearts, and he would not
> let them have power over him. No one had to tell him what
> people were like. He already knew (John 2:24,25 CEV).

Jesus knows each of us. He, therefore, can be a righteous judge.

G. HIS JUDGMENT IS FINAL

In conclusion, we also discover that the judgment of Jesus Christ is final. No appeal can be made once He has given His decision. His Word is the last word!

THERE WILL BE AN APPOINTED TIME OF JUDGMENT FOR ALL OF HUMANITY

This basically sums up what the Scriptures have to say about the future judgment of the human race. Consequently, there will be an appointed time of judgment, an appointed Judge of humanity, Jesus Christ, and an appointed purpose of judgment. Judgment by God is an appointment we all must keep!

SUMMARY TO QUESTION 19
WHO WILL BE THE JUDGE OF HUMANITY? WHAT DOES THE BIBLE SAY ABOUT JESUS JUDGING THE WORLD?

The human race will be judged someday. This is the plain teaching of Scripture. The Bible is also clear that the God of the Bible will be the judge of the world. He and He alone will judge the human race. Neither angels nor humans, nor any other created beings, are able to accomplish this. Only God has that right, as well as that ability, to judge the world.

Scripture reveals that it will be God the Son, Jesus Christ, who will be the ultimate judge of humanity. Jesus Himself testified to this fact. He said that the right to judge the world belongs to Him.

In addition, the Apostle Paul, the Apostle Peter, and John in the Book of Revelation also emphasized that Jesus will someday judge the human race. Thus, God, in the Person of Jesus Christ, will be the judge of each of us.

We should also note that believers will be judged differently than unbelievers. New Testament believers will be rewarded for the deeds which they have done after the time they believed in Jesus Christ. Old Testament believers will likewise be rewarded for their faithful service to the Lord.

Therefore, the judgment of Jesus is a time of reward for those who have trusted Him. It will be "reward day."

Unbelievers, on the other hand, will be condemned for not believing in the God of the Bible or in His Son Jesus Christ. They will be banished from His presence.

Thus, Jesus the Judge will either receive people into His kingdom or send them away from His kingdom. There is no other place where they can go.

Jesus Christ certainly has the qualifications to be the righteous judge of the human race. The Bible says that He knows what is inside the heart of each and every human being.

Therefore, He can accurately judge us. Indeed, the Bible emphasizes that Jesus will be the fair and righteous judge of all of us. He will show no partiality.

We also discover that His righteous judgment is final. No one can question His decisions or appeal to some higher authority. He is the final authority!

This is what the Scripture says will happen at some time in the future. Since God's Word always comes to pass, we can expect these judgments to take place as predicted.

His Word never fails. Judgment is coming.

What Is The Stated Purpose For God's Judgment Upon The Human Race?

The Bible says that God will judge the human race. There is no doubt about this. As far as the stated reasons as to why God will judge humanity, the Bible has the following to say.

1. JUDGMENT WILL REVEAL THE TRUE CHARACTER OF EVERYONE

The judgment of the living God will make known the true character of every human being. Indeed, everything will be known. Jesus emphasized that the day is coming when all things will be revealed. He said.

> But don't be afraid of those who threaten you. For the time is coming when everything will be revealed; all that is secret will be made public (Matthew 10:26 NLT).

All that is secret will be made public. Nothing will be hidden.

On the day of judgment, people will have to account for every word they have said. Jesus made this plain. He said.

> I can guarantee that on judgment day people will have to give an account of every careless word they say. By your words you will be declared innocent, or by your words you will be declared guilty (Matthew 12:36,37 God's Word).

Our words will justify us or they will condemn us.

Everyone will be held accountable for what they have done. Paul also wrote.

> What the law says, it says to those who are ruled by the law. Its purpose is to shut every mouth and make the whole world accountable to God (Romans 3:19 NIV).

In the Book of Ecclesiastes, it also says that everything will be judged. This includes every deed and every secret thing we do. They all will be judged.

> For God will bring every deed into judgment, with every secret thing, whether good or evil (Ecclesiastes 12:14 ESV).

At the time God judges the human race, the truth about each of us will be revealed. This means nothing will be hidden. There will be no such thing as the "perfect crime." Every wrong will be made right. Thus, evil will never win.

2. JUDGMENT WILL BE MADE PUBLIC

Those who have believed in the God of Scripture have been promised eternal life. Those who have rejected Him have been warned of eternal judgment. Destinies are determined in this life alone. Once we are dead, our fate is forever determined.

While the fate of every human will have already been determined, there is the need for a public recognition of the saved and the lost. Judgment will be public. Everyone will be publicly rewarded, or publicly condemned, for their response to God's truth. Jesus said.

> For the Son of Man is going to come in his Father's glory with his angels, and then he will reward each person according to what he has done (Matthew 16:27 NIV).

Paul wrote about the various rewards and punishments that will be given to humanity. He put it this way in his letter to the Romans.

God will reward each of us for what we have done. He will give eternal life to everyone who has patiently done what is good in the hope of receiving glory, honor, and life that lasts forever. But he will show how angry and furious he can be with every selfish person who rejects the truth and wants to do evil. All who are wicked will be punished with trouble and suffering. It doesn't matter if they are Jews or Gentiles (Romans 2:6-9 CEV).

Because of the public nature of the events, God's justice, as well as His mercy, will be demonstrated to all.

THERE IS NO CONDEMNATION FOR BELIEVERS

God's judgment will disclose the works of each of us. For the believers there will not be any condemnation. Indeed, there will only be rewards. Paul wrote to the church at Corinth about the rewards believers will receive on judgment day, or "reward day."

By the grace God has given me, I laid a foundation as a wise builder, and someone else is building on it. But each one should build with care. For no one can lay any foundation other than the one already laid, which is Jesus Christ. If anyone builds on this foundation using gold, silver, costly stones, wood, hay or straw, their work will be shown for what it is, because the Day will bring it to light. It will be revealed with fire, and the fire will test the quality of each person's work. If what has been built survives, the builder will receive a reward. If it is burned up, the builder will suffer loss but yet will be saved—even though only as one escaping through the flames. (1 Corinthians 3:10-15 NIV).

Thus, judgment day for believers is a time of reward. These rewards will be given publicly.

1. JUDGMENT WILL VINDICATE GOD'S DEALINGS TOWARD HUMANITY

Since humans first appeared upon the earth, they have falsely claimed that God has been unfair. Ultimately, judgment day will vindicate the righteousness of God. We read about this in the Book of Revelation.

> After this, I heard what sounded like a vast crowd in heaven shouting, "Praise the Lord! Salvation and glory and power belong to our God. His judgments are true and just. He has punished the great prostitute who corrupted the earth with her immorality. He has avenged the murder of his servants (Revelation 19:1-2 NLT).

When all the facts are in, God's judgment will be shown to be fair and just, or true and righteous. This is a constant theme of Scripture.

Peter wrote about how God judges impartially.

> You say that God is your Father, but God doesn't have favorites! He judges all people by what they do. So you must honor God while you live as strangers here on earth (1 Peter 1:17 CEV).

Paul also emphasized that God does not show favoritism to anyone. He stressed this point in his letter to the Romans.

> For there is no partiality with God (Romans 2:11 NKJV).

The Lord does not allow anyone to get away with evil. Paul wrote to the Colossians emphasizing that God does not show favoritism. Everyone will be fairly judged.

> Anyone who does wrong will be paid back for what he does. God treats everyone the same (Colossians 3:25 NIV).

This sums up some of the main reasons as to why the living God will judge the human race in the future.

SUMMARY TO QUESTION 20
WHAT IS THE STATED PURPOSE FOR GOD'S JUDGMENT UPON THE HUMAN RACE?

The God of the Bible is going to judge the world. The Bible clearly teaches this fact. Judgment is indeed coming.

In addition, Scripture gives a number of reasons for God's final judgment of humanity. They include the following.

First, it will show the true character of each person. Judgment will reveal who we really are. Not only will our deeds be judged, our motives behind these deeds will also be shown. Everything will be known, nothing will be hidden.

This judgment will occur publicly! God will publicly reward or punish each person for their life here upon the earth. Those who have believed in Jesus will be rewarded for deeds done after we have believed in Him, while those who have rejected Him will be punished for their unbelief. All of this will be public.

For believers, this judgment day is more aptly termed "reward day." It is a public recognition of the works we have done since the time we have believed in Jesus Christ. This is a day to which every believer should look forward.

God has often been accused of being unfair to people. However, the judgments of God will ultimately vindicate His righteous character. Everyone will realize that God always makes the right choices. This will be publicly acknowledged.

The false charges which have been made against God, His character, and His past judgments will be once and for all refuted. When all the facts are in, it will be evident that God has been more than fair.

As mentioned, this judgment will be public but there will be no suspense about where a person is going to spend eternity. That destiny will have been determined long beforehand.

On What Basis Will People Be Judged?

The Bible speaks of the fact that all humanity will be judged, and God the Son, Jesus Christ, will judge them. The judgment in the next life will be based upon the deeds done in this life. Therefore our eternal destiny is determined here on earth, not after we die.

This being true, it is important that each of us know the basis upon which we will be judged. What standard will be applied?

From a search of the Scripture, we find the standard of judgment is as follows.

1. ACCORDING TO THE TRUTH THEY HAVE RECEIVED

Each and every individual will be judged according to the information they have received. As an illustration of this, we find that Jesus compared certain cites of His day which saw His mighty miracles, to cities that God had judged in the past, which did *not* see such mighty deeds. He made the following comparison.

> Woe to you, Chorazin! Woe to you, Bethsaida! For if the miracles that were done in you had been done in Tyre and Sidon, they would have repented in sackcloth and ashes long ago! But I tell you, it will be more tolerable for Tyre and Sidon on the day of judgment than for you. And you, Capernaum, will you be exalted to heaven? You will go down to Hades.

> For if the miracles that were done in you had been done in Sodom, it would have remained until today. But I tell you, it will be more tolerable for the land of Sodom on the day of judgment than for you (Matthew 11:21-24 HCSB).

The cities which saw His great works would be judged with a higher standard than those ancient cities which did not. While each would be judged for their sin, harsher judgment would be upon those cities which Jesus Himself visited and performed His miraculous deeds.

The scriptural truth is that "to whom much has been given, much will be required." We read of Jesus saying the following.

> But the one who did not know, and did what deserved a beating, will receive a light beating. Everyone to whom much was given, of him much will be required, and from him to whom they entrusted much, they will demand the more (Luke 12:48 ESV).

The more we know, the more we are responsible for. Therefore, the judgment of God will be based upon the amount of light, or truth, which a person has received and then how they respond to it.

2. IT WILL BE ACCORDING TO ONE'S WORKS

The Bible says that each of us will be judged according to the works which we have done. Paul wrote to the Romans.

> [God] will judge all people according to what they have done . . . But there will be glory and honor and peace from God for all who do good—for the Jew first and also for the Gentile. For God does not show favoritism (Romans 2:6,10,11 NLT).

Our works will be taken into account on judgment day.

In the Book of Revelation we read of God's judgment based upon His knowledge of the minds and hearts. Thus, it is not only the outward work that will be judged but also the motivation which led to that deed. We read the following words of Jesus.

> I will kill her children with the plague. Then all the churches will know that I am the One who examines minds and hearts, and I will give to each of you according to your works (Revelation 2:23 HCSB).

The Lord knows what motivates each and every one of us. He will judge our works, our deeds, based upon this motivation that causes us to act.

WHAT IS THE WORK OF GOD?

This leads us to an important truth. Lest we might think that God will weigh our good deeds against our bad deeds, He has told us what the work of God consists.

> Then they said to Him, "What shall we do, that we may work the works of God?" Jesus answered and said to them, "This is the work of God, that you believe in Him whom He sent" (John 6:28,29 NKJV).

The work of God is to believe in Him whom He has sent, Jesus Christ. This is the one issue in which everyone will ultimately be judged; what have they done with Jesus?

3. ACCORDING TO GOD'S STANDARDS—JESUS CHRIST

Humanity will be judged according to God's standards, not ours. We will be measured against Jesus Christ; we will not be compared with one another. Indeed, the Apostle wrote about how we all fall short of God's standard, Jesus.

> For everyone has sinned; we all fall short of God's glorious standard (Romans 3:23 NLT).

God measures every human being against a perfect standard; Jesus. Obviously, none of match up very well against Him!

A. JUDGMENT IS BASED UPON ONE'S RELATIONSHIP TO CHRIST

The basis of God's judgment of each individual will be their relationship to Jesus Christ. We read the following in the Gospel of John.

> There is no judgment awaiting those who trust him. But those who do not trust him have already been judged for not believing in the only Son of God. Their judgment is based on this fact: The light from heaven came into the world, but they loved the darkness more than the light, for their actions were evil (John 3:18,19 NLT).

God has kept His promise and sent God the Son, Jesus, to earth. It is our responsibility to respond to what He has done on our behalf; dying for our sins. We must act in faith toward Him.

Those who reject Jesus Christ will be judged. Jesus made this very plain when speaking about the judgment humanity was eventually going to receive. John records Him saying.

> But there is a judge for anyone who does not accept me and my words. The very words I have spoken will judge him on the last day (John 12:48 NIV).

The words of Jesus, the truth of His claims, will be a basis for judgment. Rejection of Jesus Christ is the one sin that causes judgment.

B. SALVATION ONLY COMES BY GRACE THOUGH FAITH

Salvation, therefore, is not a matter of our good deeds; it is based upon what Jesus Christ has done for us. Paul made this as plain as anyone could when he wrote to the Ephesians. He said.

> For by grace you have been saved through faith. And this is not your own doing; it is the gift of God, not a result of works, so that no one may boast (Ephesians 2:8,9 ESV).

Salvation is by grace through faith. It is not possible for us to earn it. Paul emphasized that our good works cannot save us. He wrote to Titus.

> He saved us, not because of the righteous things we had done, but because of his mercy. He washed away our sins, giving us a new birth and new life through the Holy Spirit (Titus 3:5 NLT).

Our ultimate salvation will be based upon the grace and mercy of God. Our good deeds will have absolutely nothing to do with it.

4. THE JUDGMENT OF GOD WILL BE FAIR

Finally, we must again note that judgment of God will be fair. The psalmist wrote about the fairness of God when it comes to judgment.

> To the LORD. He is coming to judge all people on earth with fairness and truth (Psalm 96:13 CEV).

The Lord will come in judgment. When He arrives, He will judge fairly.

The Apostle Paul also emphasized this truth about the fairness of God's judgment. The Book of Acts records him saying the following.

> He [God] has set a day when he will judge the world's people with fairness. And he has chosen the man Jesus to do the judging for him. God has given proof of this to all of us by raising Jesus from death (Acts 17:31 CEV).

There is no doubt that God will be fair in His judgments. This is consistent with the character of the Lord as revealed in the Bible.

We find further evidence of the fairness of God's judgment in the Book of Jeremiah. Jeremiah quoted God as saying.

> I the LORD search the heart and examine the mind, to reward a man according to his conduct, according to what his deeds deserve (Jeremiah 17:10 NIV).

God will judge everyone in a righteous and fair manner. There will be no mistaken judgments, no room for any complaint.

In sum, God will be fair in His judgments to the human race. He will judge not only our deeds but also what motivates our deeds.

However, the ultimate standard of judgment is Jesus Christ. When compared to Him, all of us fall short. This is why we need Him as our Savior.

SUMMARY TO QUESTION 21
ON WHAT BASIS WILL PEOPLE BE JUDGED?

There will come a time when the living God, the God of the Bible, will judge every human being who has ever lived. Scripture makes this clear. It also makes clear the basis upon which each of us will be judged.

To begin with, God's judgment will be based upon the truth that each person has received. Those who have been given greater opportunities will receive the stricter judgment.

In fact, Jesus spoke of certain cities which would be more harshly judged than others. Those cities which saw His miracles, and rejected them and Him, will be judged with a harsher standard than the cities of Sodom and Gomorrah which did not see any such miracles. This illustrates the principle that "to whom much is given much will be required."

The Bible also says that judgment will be based upon our works. What we have done in this life will be fairly evaluated by the Lord.

However, Jesus said that the work of God is to believe upon Him! He is the One whom God the Father has sent into the world. Where a person spends eternity depends upon how they view the Person of Jesus Christ.

To put it simply, those who receive Christ as their Savior will not be condemned. Yet those who reject His free gift of salvation will be condemned for all eternity. There is no middle ground.

Finally, the judgment of God will be fair; no one will be able to complain about being judged in an unjust way. The righteous Judge will be merciful to those who have asked for His mercy but He will not be merciful for those who have rejected Him and His truth.

This sums up what the Scripture says about basis of the future judgment of God.

Will Believers Have Any Part Of God's Judgment?

While Jesus Christ will be the ultimate judge of the human race, the Bible also says that believers will have some part in the future judgment. This can be seen as follows.

1. BELIEVERS WILL JUDGE THE WORLD

The Bible says that believers will have some part in judging the world. Paul wrote about this to the Corinthians. He said.

> Or do you not know that the saints will judge the world? And if the world is to be judged by you, are you incompetent to try trivial cases (1 Corinthians 6:2 ESV).

The saints, or believers, will judge the world. Whether this involves taking part in the judgment at the Great White Throne, or rulership in the coming kingdom, the Bible does not say. It merely says that, in some unexplained way, we will judge the world.

2. BELIEVERS WILL JUDGE ANGELS

There is something else that the Bible promises believers, but does not explain. We are told that in the future we will judge angels. Paul wrote about this to the Corinthians.

> Don't you know that we will judge angels? Then we should be able to judge the things of this life even more (1 Corinthians 6:3 NIV).

Again, we are not told in what sense we will judge angels. In addition, we do not know if the Lord is referring to good or to bad angels.

In some way, will we be part of the judgment of evil angels? Or will believers judge, in the sense of ruling, over the righteous angels in His coming kingdom? Since we are not specifically told we will have to wait for that day when, in some sense, we will judge the angels.

3. THOSE SEATED ON THRONES WILL JUDGE, OTHERS WILL RULE

The Book of Revelation tells us that, upon the return of Jesus Christ to the world, certain people will be sitting on thrones and judging while others will be given a rulership position in His kingdom. John stated the truth in this manner.

> I saw thrones. Those who had been given authority to judge were sitting on them. I also saw the souls of those whose heads had been cut off because they had given witness for Jesus and because of God's word. They had not worshiped the beast or his statue. They had not received his mark on their foreheads or hands. They came to life and ruled with Christ for 1,000 years (Revelation 20:4 NIV).

The identity and the number of these judges is not recorded. Thus, we do not know who will judge or how many people will do the judging.

In addition, we are also told that those people who refused to take the mark of the beast during the Great Tribulation period will rule with Him during His one-thousand year millennial reign.

4. THE TWELVE APOSTLES WERE PROMISED AUTHORITY TO JUDGE

The ones seated on the thrones may be the Twelve Apostles. Jesus promised them that one day they would judge the twelve tribes of Israel. Luke records Jesus saying the following.

You have stayed with me in my time of trial. And just as my Father has granted me a Kingdom, I now grant you the right to eat and drink at my table in my Kingdom. And you will sit on thrones, judging the twelve tribes of Israel (Luke 22:29,30 NLT).

In another place, Jesus said to them.

Yes, all of you have become my followers. And so in the future world, when the Son of Man sits on his glorious throne, I promise that you will sit on twelve thrones to judge the twelve tribes of Israel (Matthew 19:28 CEV).

These twelve men will have unique authority to judge in Jesus' coming kingdom.

Therefore, we find that some aspects of the privilege of judging will be given to humans who have believed in Jesus.

SUMMARY TO QUESTION 22
WILL BELIEVERS HAVE ANY PART OF GOD'S JUDGMENT?

While the God of the Bible is to be the judge of the world in the future, the Scripture says that believers will also judge the world in some sense. However, it does not explain how this will be done. From God's Word, we do learn certain things.

The Apostle Paul told the people in Corinth that the saints, or believers, will judge the world. There is no explanation of exactly what he meant by this.

Scripture also says that we believers will judge angels. Again, no further explanation is given. The Bible does not say whether it is good or bad angels that we will judge.

If it is good angels, then it may refer to our rulership role in the coming kingdom where we would have authority over angels. However, this is only speculation.

The Bible, in the Book of Revelation, speaks of certain elders judging. We are not told who these elders are or how many of them do the judging.

Scripture also promises that those who refuse to take the mark of the beast in the Great Tribulation period will rule with Jesus in His earthly reign of 1,000 years. As to exactly what they will do, we are not told.

We know that Jesus promised the Twelve Apostles that they would be involved in judging the nation Israel. They may be these elders who will exercise this future judgment or there may be other "elders" who are not identified. We simply do not know.

Again, we do not have enough information to be certain. This is one of those areas where we must admit our ignorance. However, what is certain is that believers will have some part in the judgment process in the future.

What Arguments Are Given For People Having A Second Chance To Go To Believe After Their Death? (Post Mortem Evangelism, Second Probation)

Everyone agrees that there are people who die without having believed in Jesus Christ. Scripture as well as personal experience teaches us this. This has happened since the very beginning of the Christian era and it continues until today.

Furthermore, many of these people who die without Christ have never heard a gospel presentation. They have never have had an opportunity to accept or reject the message of Jesus Christ. Indeed, they have never heard it. What will happen to them? What is their fate?

We can add something further. There is no clear answer to this question as to the destiny of those who have never heard of Christ. Indeed, Christians give a variety of answers to this difficult issue.

In other words, there has been no consensus among Bible-believers as to how this question should be addressed. For centuries, it has been a debated question.

POST MORTEM EVANGELISM, SECOND PROBATION

This being the case, there are some Bible-believing Christians who claim that people will have a chance to receive Jesus Christ as Savior after their death. These are individuals who have never had a chance to hear the message of Christ during their lifetime. Before they are judged by the Lord, they are given an opportunity to believe in Jesus. This is known by a variety of names. These include the "gospel of the second chance," "second probation," or "post-mortem evangelism."

The support for this theory is as follows.

1. SOME HAVE DIED WITHOUT HEARING: THEY NEVER HAD A FIRST CHANCE

We know that there are many people who have died without ever having heard the name Jesus Christ. They have never had the chance to accept or reject Christ. For whatever reason, the message never got to them. This first point is not disputed by anyone.

2. PEOPLE MUST COME TO GOD THROUGH JESUS

There is something else which is plain. The Bible is also clear that salvation comes through Jesus Christ alone.

Simon Peter said the following to a group of people who had witnessed a miraculous healing in the name of Jesus.

> Salvation is found in no one else, for there is no other name under heaven given to men by which we must be saved (Acts 4:12 NIV).

Only Jesus can bring salvation to a human being. Nobody else has that ability.

Jesus Himself said that He was the one way to reach the one God. In one of the most famous statements in all of the Bible, we read of Jesus claiming to be the only way to reach the one God.

> Jesus said to him, "I am the way, and the truth, and the life. No one comes to the Father except through me" (John 14:6 NKJV).

The message of the New Testament could not be clearer. There is one way to reach the one true God and that is through the Person of Jesus Christ.

3. PEOPLE WILL BE JUDGED FOR THEIR REJECTION OF CHRIST

This brings us to our next point. The Bible speaks of a day of judgment where every human being will be brought before God and judged. The basis of this judgment is how they have responded to Jesus Christ. Those who have trusted Him will go to heaven but those who have rejected Him will be sent to an eternal hell.

But that is precisely the problem! Many people have never had a chance in this life to believe in Jesus. Nobody has ever reached them with the good news of Christ and His offer for forgiveness of sin. If they are going to be specifically condemned for rejecting Christ, then it logically follows that they must hear about Him.

If they don't hear in this life, then, of necessity, they must hear sometime after they have died. This is especially true if they are condemned to hell for not responding to the gospel.

4. THE FAIRNESS OF GOD NEEDS TO BE CONSIDERED

Consequently, since God is fair, He will give these particular individuals, the ones who have never heard of Jesus, a chance to believe in Him after their death.

Again, we stress that this is not a second chance for these lost people to believe. To the contrary, they never had the first chance to trust Christ.

If God is a fair God, a righteous God, as all agree that He is, then He must give each individual a realistic chance to accept or reject Jesus Christ. Otherwise people would be condemned for something which they had absolutely no control over. Each person must willfully reject Christ as Savior before they can be sent to hell. If not, then they are sent to hell through no fault of their own. This is inconsistent with what we know about the God of the Bible. He would not let that happen. He is the righteous Judge.

Therefore, seeing that there are many people have never heard the name of Jesus, it would be unfair of God to condemn them without a reasonable chance to believe. Consequently they must have a chance to hear the gospel of Christ presented in an understandable manner; if not in this life, then in the next.

5. GOD'S POWER EXTENDS BEYOND THE GRAVE

This is where we must appreciate the power of the God of Scripture. It is clear from His Word that His power is not limited. Death is no barrier to Him. If He desires to reach out to people with His message of forgiveness, even though they have already died, then this is His choice. Nobody tells Him what to do and He is certainly able to do this if He wishes. The Lord Himself has asked the following question.

BEHOLD, I AM THE LORD, THE GOD OF ALL FLESH: IS THERE ANY THING TOO HARD FOR ME? (JEREMIAH 32:27 KJV)

Of course, the answer is "No." Nothing is too difficult for the Lord. Therefore, the idea that He will allow a gospel message to be presented to the unbelieving dead is not inconsistent with His power. Indeed, the power of God should not be minimized. We cannot place our limitations on Him.

6. THIS PROVIDES AN ANSWER TO THE PROBLEM OF EVIL

Those who advocate post mortem evangelism actually believe that this helps answer the problem of evil as well as a number of questions about the fairness of God. Those who have not heard the gospel in this life are not sent to hell without being given a chance to respond. They are given a chance after death. This being the case, God cannot be accused of being unfair or unjust to the lost. They are lost because they choose to be lost; not because they were unreached with the gospel in this life.

This has been the complaint against the traditional view; that death ends all chances to believe. It does not seem fair that countless millions of people who have never heard of Jesus are condemned through no fault of their own. The post-mortem evangelism position does not set these limits upon God.

7. GOD DOES NOT LET OUR FAILURE STOP HIM

Another helpful thing about this theory is that it allows for God to overrule human failure. Though the church is commanded to go into the entire world and preach the gospel, we have failed miserably in this task. Not everyone has heard the good news of Jesus. While we have failed, God will not. The ones we do not reach in time, the Lord will reach in eternity. Death is no obstacle to Him.

8. THIS DOES NOT MEAN WE STOP PREACHING CHRIST

The fact that the unevangelized will have a chance to hear the gospel after they have died does not mean that we stop all missionary activity today. To the contrary, it is our marching orders from Jesus that we take this message into the entire world. His last recorded words in Matthew's gospel are as follow.

> Then Jesus came near and said to them, "All authority has been given to Me in heaven and on earth. Go, therefore, and make disciples of all nations, baptizing them in the name of the Father and of the Son and of the Holy Spirit, teaching them to observe everything I have commanded you. And remember, I am with you always, to the end of the age" (Matthew 28:18-20 HCSB).

These words should be obeyed even if the unevangelized will get a chance to hear the good news in the afterlife.

9. THIS IS NOT A NEW BELIEF

It has also been contended that there have been those who have held this belief in post-mortem evangelism since the beginning of the church era. In other words, this is not a new teaching. While everyone admits that it has not been a popular doctrine, there have been those Bible students and theologians who have held to it.

Consequently, it should not be written off as some strange new doctrine. There are Bible-believers who have held to this teaching as consistent with the rest of the Word of God.

Furthermore, the fact that it has not been more widely accepted is not troubling to those who advocate this theory. They say that this is understandable. Many doctrines which Christians now hold to be dear took some time to develop.

Indeed, the correct understanding how the members of the Godhead, God the Father, God the Son, and God the Holy Spirit, were related to each other was not settled until the fourth century.

In addition, it was not until the Protestant Reformation that the doctrine of justification by faith was properly explained. Therefore, we should not think it strange that something like the evangelization of the dead take some time to be understood by the masses.

These above points have caused a number of Bible-believers to embrace this idea of post-mortem evangelism.

WHEN WILL THEY HEAR?

There is no agreement among those who hold this belief as to when these people will hear the gospel and have a chance to trust Christ. Some feel it is immediately upon death. In other words, it will be in the intermediate state.

Others, however, believe these people will be raised from the dead and then they will make their choice.

Whatever the case may be, this theory argues that some time after the death of the person, whether shortly thereafter, or after a long period of time, they will have a chance to accept Christ as their Savior.

In sum, these are the main arguments put forward by those who believe in some sort of post-mortem evangelism.

SUMMARY TO QUESTION 23
WHAT ARGUMENTS ARE GIVEN FOR PEOPLE HAVING A SECOND CHANCE TO GO TO HEAVEN AFTER THEIR DEATH? (POST MORTEM EVANGELISM, SECOND PROBATION)

The problem of the fate of those who have never heard about Jesus Christ is one where Christians do not have a clear solution. Indeed, there are good Bible-believing Christians who offer a number of different possible answers on this difficult subject. One of the solutions offered is known as post-mortem evangelism or second probation.

The theory can be summed up as follows. We know that there are millions of people who die without ever hearing the name of Jesus while they are alive. Nobody disputes this.

We also know that it is only through Jesus that individuals can come to know the one true God. This is the message of Jesus and His apostles. There is no doubt that this is what they taught.

The Bible also speaks of a day when the Lord will judge the world for their rejection of Christ. Judgment day is coming. Again, this is something which all believers agree upon.

This being the case, it seems that people must have a chance to hear about Christ before they can be condemned to endless punishment for rejecting Him. If they do not hear in this life, then they must hear sometime after their death and before the last judgment.

Otherwise it seems that God would not be fair. He would be condemning them for something which, by definition, they could not do. It should be noted that this is not really a "gospel of the second chance" but rather a first chance for these lost people to believe.

This position also emphasizes the fairness of God. Again, this a doctrine which everyone acknowledges that the Scripture clearly teaches. The God of Scripture is a fair or just Judge. While we would not condemn someone in this life for something which was beyond their control, why should we assume that the Lord, the just Judge, will do this to those who have not heard about Jesus? It is not their fault that a Christian did not reach them with the gospel.

Will the Lord then condemn them for something they were not able to do; to believe in Jesus? This theory says He will not. Before they can be sent to eternal punishment, they must willingly and knowingly reject the message of Christ. They receive this chance after death if they did not have the chance while alive here upon the earth.

The fact that the lost can be reached with the gospel is not something which is beyond God's power. He is able to reach anyone whom He chooses. This includes the dead.

Post-mortem evangelism also helps us with an answer to the problem of evil. No longer can anyone accuse God of being powerless to do anything about evil or uncaring to the place which He does not do anything about it. He actually goes the "extra mile" in allowing everyone to hear the message of Jesus Christ before the judgment. Whether in this life, or in the next, they will have the chance to respond before the Day of Judgment.

The fact that the Lord may reach out beyond the grave to evangelize those who have never heard about Jesus does not mean that we should stop all missionary activity. We should not. In obedience to Christ we should maintain the urgency to bring the good news of Christ to the entire world. This is still our responsibility.

While this idea may seem strange to the ears of many people, it is not something which is new in the history of the church. There have been a number of Bible students who have held a view such as this.

Furthermore, we should not reject it out of hand simply because the majority of believers and Bible teachers have not embraced it. Indeed, it took a number of centuries for Christians to gain a proper understanding of the relationship between God the Father, God the Son, and God the Holy Spirit; the Trinity. Through much study and reflection a more complete understanding of the nature of the God of the Bible was reached. But it did not happen right away.

In the same manner, it was not until the Protestant Reformation that the doctrine of justification by faith was made clear. Again, it took centuries for the church to come to an understanding of this particular truth.

Therefore, we should not discard the idea of evangelizing the dead who have never had a chance to hear about Christ. It should at least be up for discussion. New ideas about biblical doctrines sometimes take a long time before they are properly understood and appreciated.

As to exactly when this evangelism of the dead occurs is not certain. It will happen at some point in the intermediate state. This represents the time between the death of that person and the final judgment. It is sometime within this period that post-mortem evangelism will occur. Beyond that, nobody can be certain.

This sums up the case for the post-mortem, or "after death evangelism" of those who have never heard about Jesus. While it is not a well-known or even a popular belief among Bible-believing Christians, it is being proclaimed by a number of people.

Does The Bible Teach A Second Chance To Be Saved After Death?

Is there second chance for people who have died without believing in Christ to believe in Him in the afterlife? Will God give anyone an opportunity to believe in Christ once this life is over?

While many people teach this is what will happen, the Bible says otherwise. The following points need to be made.

AFTER DEATH THERE IS JUDGMENT, NOT PROBATION

To begin with, the Bible says that after death comes the judgment for people. There is not some type of probation for those who did not believe in this life; whatever their situation may have been. The writer to the Hebrews said.

> And just as it is appointed for people to die once—and after this, judgment (Hebrews 9:27 HCSB).

The New Living Translation translates the verse in this manner.

> And just as it is destined that each person dies only once and after that comes judgment (Hebrews 9:27 NLT).

Judgment comes after death, not a chance to believe in Jesus Christ. This is taught consistently throughout the Scripture.

THE ETERNAL STATE OF UNBELIEVERS IS DETERMINED IN THIS LIFE ALONE

The Bible is clear that the eternal state of all of us, our ultimate destiny, is dependent upon what we do in this life, and in this life alone. Jesus said to the religious leaders of His day that they will die in their sins if they do not believe in Him.

> I told you that you would die in your sins; if you do not believe that I am he, you will indeed die in your sins (John 8:24 NIV).

These religious leaders were no different than any other human being. Each and every person who dies without Jesus Christ is forever lost. Jesus gives no indication that they, or anyone else, can have some type of chance to believe in the afterlife.

THE TIME OF SALVATION IS NOW

The Bible urges people to believe in God's promises because the time of salvation is now. Indeed, it is not some time after this life is over. Paul wrote.

> For God says, "At just the right time, I heard you. On the day of salvation, I helped you." Indeed, God is ready to help you right now. Today is the day of salvation (2 Corinthians 6:2 NLT).

Salvation needs to happen right now. It should never be put off until later; certainly not until someone gets to the next life.

THERE IS A FIXED STATE AFTER DEATH

There is something else. The Bible also says that the state of the dead is forever fixed. In the story that Jesus gave of the rich man and Lazarus, the gulf between the believing and unbelieving dead was explained in the following manner.

And besides, there is a great chasm separating us. Anyone who wanted to cross over to you from here is stopped at its edge, and no one there can cross over to us (Luke 16:26 NLT).

After death, the eternal state for the person is fixed; no change is possible. There is no chance of crossing over.

GOD DETERMINES WHAT IS FAIR

Finally, we want to emphasize that it is God of the Bible that determines what is fair and what is not fair, it is not sinful human beings who decide this question. It is wrong to accuse God of unfairness because of what we think He should do. The Bible says the following about God's character.

Who can ever understand what is in the LORD's mind? Who can ever give him advice. Did the LORD have to ask anyone to help him understand? Did he have to ask someone to teach him the right way?

Who taught him what he knows? Who showed him how to understand (Isaiah 40:13,14 NIV).

The translation "God's Word" puts it this way.

Who has directed the Spirit of the Lord or instructed him as his adviser? Whom did he consult? Who gave him understanding? Who taught him the right way? Who taught him knowledge? Who informed him about the way to understanding (Isaiah 40:13,14 God's Word).

The answer to this question, of course, is nobody. Nobody directs God and nobody tells Him what to do. He is the One who makes all the decisions.

Paul also made this same point very clear. God does exactly what He wants to do. He wrote the following to the Romans.

> But who are you, O man, to talk back to God? "Shall what
> is formed say to him who formed it, 'Why did you make me
> like this?'" (Romans 9:20 NIV).

Indeed, who are we to question God? He formed us. He knows what
is best. We certainly do not. Therefore, we need to trust Him on all
decisions.

Hence, God is the one who determines what is, and what is not
fair, it is not the responsibility of fallible human beings to make this
determination.

GOD WILL JUDGE EVERYONE RIGHTEOUSLY

There is one other point which we need to make. The Bible says that
when the Lord eventually judges the world He will do it righteously
or with fairness. Indeed, He is the righteous Judge of the entire earth.

The Apostle Paul said the following to a group of people who had gathered in Athens to hear about the God whom he preached.

> Therefore, having overlooked the times of ignorance, God
> now commands all people everywhere to repent, because He
> has set a day on which He is going to judge the world in
> righteousness by the Man He has appointed. He has pro-
> vided proof of this to everyone by raising Him from the dead
> (Acts 17:30-31 HCSB).

According to this statement, when the God of the Bible judges the
human race, everyone will receive fair treatment. Everyone will be
treated and judged righteously. Even though we may not know exactly
how He will do it with certain people, this statement from Paul should
settle the matter for all Bible-believers.

Consequently, we conclude from the totality of evidence in the Bible
that God does not give humans a chance to believe after they have died.
This life is all that there is as far as determining our ultimate destiny.

SUMMARY TO QUESTION 24
DOES THE BIBLE TEACH A SECOND CHANCE TO BE SAVED AFTER DEATH?

Many think that the Lord will give the lost a chance to believe after death. For whatever reason, God will not make this life to be their only hope. They will have an opportunity to believe in the afterlife. This is held for a number of reasons.

For one thing, this will actually be a first chance for belief for some. Indeed, millions of people have died without ever hearing the name of Jesus Christ. It has been argued that the Lord will give them an opportunity to trust Christ some time after their death but before the Final Judgment. Many conclude this because from our perspective it seems to be the only fair way of dealing with these people.

However, the idea, that God will give people a chance to believe after death, while popular, is certainly not taught in Scripture. To the contrary, the Bible emphasizes that "today" is the day of salvation because there is no chance after death.

Scripture teaches that after the death of each and every human being there is only judgment which awaits them. There is no probation, no other opportunity to believe. The future of an individual is determined in this life and in this life alone.

As for those that argue that this is unfair, let us remember that God alone determines what is fair. He is a righteous God. Scripture emphasizes that there is no injustice in Him. We need to trust the Lord that whatever happens to each and every human being will be fairly and righteously decided by Him.

Indeed, we are specifically told that when the Lord judges the world, He will do it righteously. That should settle the issue. In whatever way that He will judge the lost, He will do it fairly. Nobody will be able to object to their ultimate fate.

What Are The Various Judgments That Are Still To Come?

While the God of the Bible has judged the world in the past, and is presently judging the world, the Bible says that God will also judge in the future. Scripture promises that the living God will judge humanity, angels, and our fallen world.

The Bible speaks of the following judgments that are still to come.

1. THE JUDGMENT SEAT OF CHRIST, THE JUDGMENT SEAT OF GOD

This judgment concerns only New Testament believers. They will receive rewards for their faithfulness to Jesus Christ. They will be judged in the sense of rewards, not condemnation. We read about this in two different places in Scripture.

> For we must all appear before the judgment seat of Christ, so that each of us may receive what is due us for the things done while in the body, whether good or bad (2 Corinthians 5:10 NIV).

In Romans, Paul called this the judgment seat of God, or the tribunal of God.

> Why do you criticize or despise other Christians? Everyone will stand in front of God to be judged. Scripture says, "As certainly as I live, says the Lord, everyone will worship me,

and everyone will praise God." All of us will have to give an account of ourselves to God. So let's stop criticizing each other. Instead, you should decide never to do anything that would make other Christians have doubts or lose their faith (Romans 14:10-13 God's Word).

In this passage, the Apostle Paul indicated the personal responsibility of every Christian. Indeed, we are to "give an account of ourselves to God." Notice that none of us will have to answer for the behavior of fellow Christians. However, we will have to account for what we have said and done.

These rewards will be for deeds done after the person has believed in Jesus. Judgment day will be "reward day." These rewards will be earned *after* they have trusted Christ in faith.

2. JUDGMENT OF LIVING ISRAEL

When Jesus Christ returns, He will judge the living members of the nation Israel. Those who have trusted Him will enter His earthly kingdom and will be with Christ for all eternity. Those who do not trust Him will be condemned. We read of this in the Book of Ezekiel.

> As I judged your ancestors in the wilderness of the land of Egypt, so I will judge you, declares the Sovereign Lord. I will take note of you as you pass under my rod, and I will bring you into the bond of the covenant. I will purge you of those who revolt and rebel against me. Although I will bring them out of the land where they are living, yet they will not enter the land of Israel. Then you will know that I am the Lord (Ezekiel 20:36-38 NIV).

Consequently, the nation of Israel will receive their own unique judgment at the return of the Lord.

3. JUDGMENT OF THE GENTILES

The Gentiles, or non-Jews, will also be judged when Jesus Christ returns. Those who have trusted Christ will enter His earthly kingdom, while those who have not will be taken to judgment. Jesus spoke of this judgment.

> When the Son of Man comes in his glory, and all the angels with him, he will sit on his glorious throne. All the nations will be gathered before him, and he will separate the people one from another as a shepherd separates the sheep from the goats. He will put the sheep on his right and the goats on his left (Matthew 25:31-32 NIV).

The nations will be judged upon the return of the Lord.

4. THE JUDGMENT OF THE OLD TESTAMENT SAINTS

The Old Testament believers will be raised from the dead when Christ returns. They will be rewarded for their faithfulness to Him and will inherit the promises of the kingdom. Scripture says their bodies will be awakened from their sleep of death to enter the kingdom.

> At that time Michael, the great prince who protects your people, will arise. There will be a time of distress such as has not happened from the beginning of nations until then. But at that time your people—everyone whose name is found written in the book —will be delivered. Multitudes who sleep in the dust of the earth will awake: some to everlasting life . . . (Daniel 12:1-2 NIV).

The bodies of the believers from the Old Testament era will be raised to everlasting life.

5. JUDGMENT OF THE TRIBULATION SAINTS

There will be those who die during the Great Tribulation who trust Christ before their death. Christ will judge them when He returns.

This judgment will not be one of condemnation but of reward since there is no condemnation for those who are in Christ Jesus.

> Then I saw thrones, and people seated on them who were given authority to judge. I also saw the people who had been beheaded because of their testimony about Jesus and because of God's word, who had not worshiped the beast or his image, and who had not accepted the mark on their foreheads or their hands. They came to life and reigned with the Messiah for 1,000 years (Revelation 20:4 HCSB).

These believers will rule and reign with Christ.

6. THE JUDGMENT OF THE BEAST AND THE FALSE PROPHET

There will also be a judgment of the beast, also known as the man of sin, the Antichrist, as well as his promoter, the false prophet. We are told that each of them will be thrown into the lake of fire upon the return of Jesus Christ to the earth.

> The beast and the false prophet who had done miracles for the beast were captured. By these miracles the false prophet had deceived those who had the brand of the beast and worshiped its statue. Both of them were thrown alive into the fiery lake of burning sulfur (Revelation 19:20 God's Word).

They will spend eternity in the "lake of fire."

7. JUDGMENT OF SATAN

Christ will also judge Satan, the created spirit-being who became the devil, when He returns to the earth and sets up His kingdom. He will be sent to the bottomless pit and eventually to the lake of fire. His judgment is certain.

> The Devil who deceived them was thrown into the lake of fire and sulfur where the beast and the false prophet are,

and they will be tormented day and night forever and ever (Revelation 20:10 HCSB).

He will be judged forever in this "lake of fire."

8. JUDGMENT OF FALLEN ANGELS

The evil angels who followed Satan will receive their judgment after Christ returns to our world. They will be condemned and punished for all eternity. Jesus spoke of their coming judgment.

> Then the king will say to those on his left, 'Get away from me! God has cursed you! Go into everlasting fire that was prepared for the devil and his angels (Matthew 25:41 God's Word).

We find that the "everlasting fire" was prepared for the devil as well as for his angels. As to the exact timing of their judgment, Scripture does not tell us. It may happen at His Second Coming or it may take place one thousand years later at the Great White Throne judgment.

9. JUDGMENT OF THE UNSAVED DEAD

At the Great White Throne Judgment, the unsaved dead from all time will be judged and sent to their final destination by the One whom they rejected. This destination is hell, the lake of fire. We read of this in the Book of Revelation.

> I saw a large, white throne and the one who was sitting on it. The earth and the sky fled from his presence, but no place was found for them. I saw the dead, both important and unimportant people, standing in front of the throne. Books were opened, including the Book of Life. The dead were judged on the basis of what they had done, as recorded in the books. The sea gave up its dead. Death and hell gave up their dead. People were judged based on what they had done. Death and hell were thrown into the fiery lake.

(The fiery lake is the second death.) Those whose names were not found in the Book of Life were thrown into the fiery lake (Revelation 20:11-15 God's Word).

10. JUDGMENT OF THE MILLENNIAL BELIEVERS

During the thousand year reign of Christ on the earth, known as the Millennium, there will be people who are born to those who have entered this kingdom age at its very beginning. These people will have a choice concerning Jesus Christ. They can believe in Him or they can reject Him.

Those who have trusted Christ during the Millennium will be rewarded. While Scripture doesn't tell us when or where this will take place, it is most likely at the Great White Throne Judgment.

11. JUDGMENT OF DEATH AND HADES

Death and Hades, the intermediate realm of the dead, will also be judged and thrown into the lake of fire. Therefore, there will be an end of death and there will not be an in-between place where the dead reside. Everyone will be at their ultimate destination.

> Death and Hades were thrown into the lake of fire. This is the second death, the lake of fire (Revelation 20:13 HCSB).

Death will be no more, neither will there be any "in-between place" of the dead.

12. JUDGMENT OF THE PRESENT HEAVENS AND EARTH

Finally, God will judge the present heavens and the earth. The Lord will then make a new heaven and new earth.

> I saw a new heaven and a new earth, because the first heaven and earth had disappeared, and the sea was gone (Revelation 21:1 God's Word).

These are the specific judgments which are still to come. As we can readily observe there are many judgments which remain in the future.

NOTE: THERE ARE DIFFERENCES AMONG BELIEVERS ABOUT THESE COMING JUDGMENTS

We should note here that there are differences among believers with respect to these judgments. Some Bible-believers do not think that there will be this many separate judgments.

Indeed, they argue that the dead will be judged in one final judgment when the Lord returns. Usually those who hold this view do not believe that there will be a literal thousand year reign of Christ on the earth, a Millennium.

Therefore, there will be no millennial saints to judge. We will explain why these various views are held in the coming questions.

SUMMARY TO QUESTION 25
WHAT ARE THE VARIOUS JUDGMENTS THAT ARE STILL TO COME?

There are a number of judgments that the Bible speaks about that are still to come. We can sum them up as follows.

One of the future judgments which is coming is known as the judgment seat of Christ or the judgment seat of God. This is where New Testament believers are rewarded for their faithfulness to Him. This will be a time of rewards, not condemnation.

Those who are alive from the nation Israel, as well as those from among the Gentiles nations, will be judged at the Second Coming of Christ.

There will also be a resurrection and judgment of Old Testament saints when Christ returns. They will enter into His promised kingdom.

During the period of the Great Tribulation, many will believe in Christ. However, a number of them will suffer martyrdom for their belief. They too will be raised and rewarded at the Second Coming of Christ.

There will be a judgment of the man of sin, the Antichrist, as well as his cohort, the false prophet, when Christ returns. They will be thrown alive into the lake of fire.

Satan and his fallen angels will also be judged. They will be cast into the lake of fire where they have to suffer endlessly for their rebellion against the Lord.

There will also be a final judgment for all unbelievers. This is known as the Great White Throne Judgment. After the millennial reign of Christ, these unbelievers will be judged before the Lord. Since their names are not written in the Book of Life, they will be thrown into the lake of fire where they have to suffer eternally.

The people who have been born during the millennial reign of Christ and have trusted Him as their Savior will, most-likely, also be rewarded at this time. However, they will not be condemned but rather rewarded.

Death itself will be judged as will the intermediate state of the dead, Hades. They will be thrown into the lake of fire and hence will no longer exist.

Finally, the present heavens and earth will be judged and a new heaven and new earth will be created.

We note that not all Christians see this many specific judgments in the future. Instead they lump many of them together into one great "Judgment Day." This position is often held by those who do not believe Scripture teaches that there will be a literal Millennium, a thousand year reign of Christ upon the earth.

What Are The Arguments For Everyone Being Judged At Once? (One General Judgment)

In the future, God will judge humanity, angels, and our fallen world. Of this, there is no doubt. There are, however, different perspectives on when these judgments will happen. Some believe it will happen all at once while others believe it will happen in stages.

THE EXACT TIME OF JUDGMENT IS NOT CERTAIN FOR SOME

While many people believe that the world will experience only one day of judgment in the future, "Judgment Day," those who believe it will happen all at once, are divided as to when it will occur.

There are some believers who think it will happen at the time of the Second Coming of Jesus Christ. When He returns to the earth all the promised judgments will take place at that time.

Others believe that after the Second Coming of Christ there will be a literal thousand year reign of Christ on the earth, a Millennium. At the end of this one thousand year period there will be the one, final judgment. This is also known as the "Last Judgment." This is the judgment day Scripture is speaking of.

Whatever the exact time may be, it is believed that all of these judgments will occur at the same time according to those who hold this perspective.

THE CASE FOR ONLY ONE JUDGMENT

Those who believe that the Bible teaches only one judgment, rather than a number of separate judgments, reason as follows.

1. THE BIBLE SPEAKS OF ONE JUDGMENT DAY

To begin with, there are many passages that speak of a "day" of judgment. If we are to take the Bible literally, then we should understand a day as a day. It is not an extended period of time.

JESUS SPOKE OF JUDGMENT DAY

For example, Jesus specifically said that there would be a "day" of judgment in which Sodom and Gomorrah would be judged.

> I assure you: It will be more tolerable on the day of judgment for the land of Sodom and Gomorrah than for that town (Matthew 10:15 HCSB).

Here Jesus spoke of the "day" of judgment. This seems to refer to one particular day; not something which is extended over a period of time.

MARTHA SPOKE OF THE LAST DAY

Martha, the sister of the dead man Lazarus spoke of a resurrection day. This would occur on the "last day."

> Jesus said to her, "Your brother will rise again." Martha answered, "I know he will rise again in the resurrection at the last day" (John 11:23,24 NIV).

While judgment is not mentioned in this context, it does speak of the "last day." Furthermore, the Scriptures always link resurrection and judgment.

PETER WROTE OF JUDGMENT DAY

Peter also wrote of "judgment day" which is to come. He made the point that the unrighteous are presently kept under punishment as they wait for this particular day.

If this is so, then the Lord knows how to rescue the godly from trials and to hold the unrighteous for punishment on the day of judgment (2 Peter 2:9 NIV).

Again, judgment is limited to one day.

Elsewhere in the writings of Peter, we again read of the coming judgment day. On this particular day, the present heaven and earth will be destroyed. He wrote.

But by the same word, the present heavens and earth are stored up for fire, being kept until the day of judgment and destruction of ungodly men (2 Peter 3:7 HCSB).

This is another instance of a biblical reference to a judgment day. The normal way to understand this, and similar passages, is that it is speaking of one particular day.

PAUL

The Apostle Paul also spoke of a "day" when God would judge the world. He said the following to a group of people who had gathered on Mars Hill in the city of Athens.

God overlooked people's former ignorance about these things, but now he commands everyone everywhere to turn away from idols and turn to him. For he has set a day for judging the world with justice by the man he has appointed, and he proved to everyone who this is by raising him from the dead (Acts 17:30,31 NLT).

This is a further reference, from another New Testament writer, to a day of judgment. Seemingly, they are united in their teaching that there will be only one "day" of judgment.

2. THERE WILL BE A DAY OF WRATH

Scripture also describes this coming day of judgment as the "day of God's wrath." When Paul wrote to the Romans, he said the following.

But because of your hardness and unrepentant heart you are storing up wrath for yourself in the day of wrath, when God's righteous judgment is revealed (Romans 2:5 HCSB).

Therefore, it is the united testimony of Scripture that there will be one day, not many days, in which God judges the world

3. MATTHEW 25 IS A DESCRIPTION OF THE FINAL JUDGMENT

While some see Matthew 25:31-46 as a description of the judgment of certain people entering the Millennium, the thousand year reign of Jesus Christ on the earth, others think it speaks of the final judgment. A number of reasons are given. They include the following.

JESUS SPOKE OF ETERNAL PUNISHMENT AND REWARDS

The passage speaks of people going to their eternal reward, not their temporal one. The subject is their eternal destiny. It is contended that this is inconsistent with the idea that they are entering an earthly kingdom. Jesus describes it this way.

Then he will say to those on his left, 'Depart from me, you who are cursed, into the eternal fire prepared for the devil and his angels. . . . Then they will go away to eternal punishment, but the righteous to eternal life (Matthew 25:41,46 NIV).

Since eternal destinies are in view, it is more consistent to see this as the final judgment rather than to see who will, and who will not, enter a one-thousand year earthly kingdom.

NO ONE IS SAID TO BE GOING INTO THE MILLENNIUM

In addition, nothing is specifically said in this passage about believers going into a literal Millennium. The passage merely says they are entering God's kingdom. Again, we read Jesus saying.

Then the King will say to those on his right, 'Come, you who are blessed by my Father; take your inheritance, the kingdom prepared for you since the creation of the world (Matthew 25:34 NIV).

This kingdom has been prepared before the world was created. Consequently, it is more in keeping with the overall plan of God to see this as His eternal kingdom; not some one thousand year period before eternity begins.

GOD JUDGES INDIVIDUALS, NOT NATIONS

Some see an inconsistency with the rest of Scripture if this judgment recorded in Matthew 25 refers to a mere earthly kingdom. The God of the Bible judges individuals, not nations. He would not hold someone responsible for what the leaders of a particular nation did.

Therefore, it is contended, that the evidence from the Bible is clear: there will be one day in which God will judge the world.

SUMMARY TO QUESTION 26
WHAT ARE THE ARGUMENTS FOR EVERYONE BEING JUDGED AT ONCE? (ONE GENERAL JUDGMENT)

The Bible says that God will one day judge the world. There is no doubt about this. However, believers are divided as to whether there will be one general judgment or a number of different judgments in the future.

Those who argue for one general judgment emphasize that the Bible speaks of a "judgment day." This seems to indicate that everything happens on one particular day.

For example, we find Jesus speaking of a "day" of judgment. He said it will occur on one particular day.

Furthermore, Martha, the sister of Lazarus, believed that her dead brother would be raised on "the last day." Since resurrection and judgment are always linked, this must mean it will all happen on one day.

Peter also wrote about a day of judgment. On that day, the present heaven and earth will be destroyed while a new heaven and earth will be created.

In speaking to a crowd in Athens, the Apostle Paul, likewise spoke of a "judgment day."

These passages seem to make it clear that judgment will occur at one time and on one particular day.

Scripture also speaks of the "day" of God's wrath. Again, this speaks of one specific day which the Lord will judge the unbelievers. It does not indicate any time interval between judgments.

When Jesus spoke of the judgment of the nations, as recorded by Matthew, it is seen as the same event which John spoke of in the Book of Revelation; the Great White Throne Judgment. There does not seem to be any difference between the two. Everyone appears before the Judge and each person receives their proper judgment. The righteous enter into His kingdom while the unrighteous are sent away from His presence.

Furthermore, the rewards people will receive at this judgment of the nations are eternal rewards, not temporal ones. There is nothing which speaks of them going into a literal earthly kingdom, a Millennium. This is another indication that this judgment is the same as the Great White Throne Judgment.

These are some of the reasons as to why many people view the Scripture as speaking of one final judgment of the human race in which everyone participates.

Why Do People Believe There Will Be A Number Of Judgments Instead Of One Final Judgment? (Judgment Will Be In Stages)

While many Bible-believers think there will be one "Judgment Day" where each and every person who has ever lived will be judged, there is also the perspective that the various judgments, which the Scripture says will occur, will happen in stages. In other words, all judgment will not take place on one specific day. Those who believe in a number of judgments usually see it occurring it this manner.

IT BEGINS WITH THE JUDGMENT SEAT OF CHRIST

First, there will be the time when believers in Jesus Christ receive their rewards for faithful service. This occurs at the Judgment Seat of Christ which takes place before the His Second Coming.

At the Second Coming of Christ, the Lord then judges those living from the nation of Israel, the living from the Gentile nations, those who have believed in Him during the period of the Great Tribulation (the tribulation saints) and the Old Testament saints. After this judgment, the thousand year rule of Christ upon the earth begins, the Millennium.

At the end of the Millennium there will be a final judgment. This judgment will include Satan, the fallen angels, the unsaved dead from all time. Those who have believed in Jesus Christ during the Millennium will be rewarded at that time. Death and Hades, as well as the present sinful heavens and earth, will also be judged.

Therefore, according to this perspective, it is not correct to speak of one great "Judgment Day."

Those who believe in a series of judgments respond to the idea of one general judgment in the following way.

1. THE JUDGMENT IS NOT LIMITED TO ONE DAY

While the Bible does speak of judgment day, we should not assume that all judgment would take place at the same time. For example, when Paul speaks of the believer's judgment it uses the word "bema." This word often speaks of a place where rewards are given out. Thus, for believers, Judgment day is "reward day."

However a "Great White Throne" symbolizes the judgment for unbelievers. Condemnation, not rewards, is in view. Hence two different judgments are in mind.

In addition, the passages that speak of a Day of Judgment are usually in the context of speaking to unbelievers; they will be judged on that final day. Yet this is not the case with those who believe in Jesus Christ.

THE GREEK WORD TRANSLATED DAY CAN MEAN VARIOUS THINGS

Also, the Greek word translated "day" in the Bible is used in a number of different senses. In other words, it is not necessarily speaking of a single twenty-four hour period. The context must also determine what is meant.

For example, Peter spoke of an "eternal day" or the "day of eternity."

> But grow in the grace and knowledge of our Lord and Savior Jesus Christ. To him be the honor both now and on that eternal day (2 Peter 3:18 NET).

The ESV puts it this way.

> But grow in the grace and knowledge of our Lord and Savior
> Jesus Christ. To him be the glory both now and to the day of
> eternity. Amen (2 (Peter 3:18 ESV).

The "day" of eternity is another way of saying the "time of eternity."
Indeed, it not merely one specific twenty-four hour period which is in
mind!

2. MATTHEW 25 SPEAKS ABOUT AN EARTHLY KINGDOM

Matthew 25, it is argued, speaks of an earthly kingdom. While the
people are said to have entered into eternal life, or eternal judgment,
nothing is said that they were immediately sent there; either to heaven
or to hell.

In fact, we discover that eternal life begins for the believer the moment
they trust Jesus as Savior. Jesus said.

> This is eternal life: that they may know You, the only true
> God, and the One You have sent —Jesus Christ (John 17:3
> HCSB).

On the other hand, those who are lost are already in a state of condemnation. We read about this in the Gospel of John. It says the following.

> Anyone who believes in Him is not condemned, but anyone
> who does not believe is already condemned, because he has
> not believed in the name of the One and Only Son of God
> (John 3:18 HCSB).

They do not become lost; they are already lost. They need to be saved.

A few other points need to be made.

A. THE MILLENNIUM IS PART OF THE KINGDOM

While it is true that nothing is said about the Millennium in this context, it is also true that the word Millennium is not found in the entire Bible. However, in Revelation Chapter 20, we find seven specific references to a one thousand year rule of Jesus Christ upon the earth. So while the specific word may not be used, the idea is certainly there.

Consequently, the Millennium is seen as one part of the eternal kingdom; it begins the physical rule of Jesus Christ over the universe.

B. INDIVIDUALS, NOT NATIONS WILL BE JUDGED

The last objection is based upon a fallacy. Those who hold to separate judgments do not believe that entire nations will either go into the Millennium or straight to judgment. It is the "individuals" from these nations that will go into the kingdom or straight to judgment. The judgment is upon individuals from the various nations, it is not the nations themselves.

Therefore, the idea that the judgment of humanity will be in stages is not contrary to what the Scripture says.

WE SHOULD DISAGREE AGREEABLY

As there are good Bible-believing Christians on each side of this question concerning the timing of the coming judgments, we should hold our position with love and respect for others. These issues should be discussed and debated but always in a spirit of Christian love and understanding.

SUMMARY TO QUESTION 27
WHY DO PEOPLE BELIEVE THERE WILL BE A NUMBER OF JUDGMENTS INSTEAD OF ONE FINAL JUDGMENT? (JUDGMENT WILL BE IN STAGES)

There are differences of opinion among Bible-believers about the timing of the various judgments which the Bible says will occur in the future. There are two basic perspectives. Some think these judgments will occur in stages while others think they happen all at once. In other words, there will be a judgment "day."

Those who think there will be one day of judgment are not in agreement as to when this will happen. Some believe it will happen at the Second Coming of Christ while others think it will happen at the end of a thousand year reign of Christ on the earth, the Millennium. While they differ in the timing of this Last Judgment, they all agree that judgment of the entire human race will happen at one time.

The people who believe that judgment will happen in stages usually see the events unfolding in this manner.

First, there is the judgment seat of Christ where all believers in Jesus are brought together before Him. This is a time of rewards, not condemnation. It is limited to those people who have believed in Jesus during the age of the church. This takes place years before Christ returns to the earth. Indeed, it occurs at the rapture of the church.

Next, they see a judgment at the Second Coming of Christ. At that time, a number of groups are judged. This includes those from the nation of Israel as well as people from the Gentile nations of the world. This judgment is to determine who will enter the earthly kingdom of Christ, the Millennium.

Those alive at the time of the Second Coming of Christ, and who have believed in Him will enter this earthly kingdom. However, those among Israel and the Gentiles, who are unbelievers when Christ returns, will receive a death sentence. Yet, it will not be their final judgment.

There will also be a group of people who have believed in Jesus Christ during the period of the Great Tribulation, or the tribulation saints. They too will be judged at this time but their judgment is one of reward.

It is at this time that the Old Testament saints are raised from the dead and given their promised reward from the Lord.

The final judgment will occur at the Great White Throne. This will take place one thousand years later after the earthly rule of Christ upon the earth, the Millennium. All of the unbelievers from the beginning of time are raised from the dead and then judged. They will be sent away to the lake of fire.

Those who have grown up during the Millennium and have believed in Jesus Christ will most likely be judged at this time. They will be given new bodies and will enter the eternal kingdom. There is no condemnation for them.

Those who believe that there will be only one judgment day, point to the passages which speak of a "day" of judgment. Also, they emphasize that when Jesus returns and judges the nations He said that believers would go to everlasting life while unbelievers went to everlasting punishment. This does not speak of a temporal judgment but of an eternal judgment. It is much more consistent to see this occurring at a judgment "day."

In addition, they note that the kingdom promised, at the judgment of the nations, was prepared before the foundation of the world. This, they believe, speaks of an eternal kingdom.

Those who see separate judgments in Scripture do not find these objections as convincing. They respond by saying that the word "day" does not necessarily refer to one particular day but can mean a "judgment period."

In fact, the Greek word translated "day" is used in a number of different ways in Scripture. In sum, it does not always refer to one specific twenty-four hour period.

Answering another objection, the fact that some are judged to everlasting life and others to everlasting contempt at the Second Coming of Christ only means that their destinies cannot be change. Indeed, it does not necessarily mean that it would happen at that moment.

It is also contend that the Millennium is one part of the everlasting kingdom that was prepared before the world was formed. Therefore, we do not have to assume there is only one particular day of judgment.

We emphasize that each view, about the time of future judgment, is held by good Bible-believers. Whatever position one holds on this issue should be held with love towards those who differ. Indeed, they may have the right answer!

How Will Believers Be Judged?
(The Judgment Seat Of Christ: The Bema)

Greek, like English, uses the word "judge" in two senses. One sense is condemnation, while the other sense is the giving out of rewards. The Bible says unbelievers will be judged in the first sense. In other words, it speaks of their condemnation.

On the other hand, believers will be judged in a different sense, rewards. The following observations need to be made.

THERE IS A JUDGMENT SEAT OF GOD FOR BELIEVERS

The Bible speaks of a special judgment that God will hold for believers only. It is known as the judgment seat of Christ, or the judgment seat of God. Paul wrote.

> For we must all appear before the judgment seat of Christ, so that each of us may receive what is due us for the things done while in the body, whether good or bad (2 Corinthians 5:10 NIV).

All believers will stand before God and be individually judged. According to Paul, the purpose of this judgment is to receive rewards.

Paul wrote to the Romans about this judgment seat of God. He said each of us who have believed in Jesus will stand before Him.

Why do you pass judgment on your brother? Or you, why do you despise your brother? For we will all stand before the judgment seat of God (Romans 14:10 ESV).

Every believer will one day stand in His presence; before God's judgment seat.

THE JUDGMENT SEAT: THE BEMA

The judgment seat is known as the "bema." The word is also translated "court" or "tribunal." It could be a public judgment place as in the case with Pontius Pilate and Jesus. We read of this judge's seat in the Gospel of John.

When Pilate heard this, he brought Jesus out and sat down on the judge's seat at a place known as the Stone Pavement (which in Aramaic is Gabbatha) (John 19:13 NIV).

Pilate sat down on the bema, the judge's seat.

Later the Apostle Paul appeared before Festus the governor.

Festus stayed in Jerusalem for eight or ten more days before going to Caesarea. Then the next day he took his place as judge and had Paul brought into court (Acts 25:6 NIV).

The phrase translated "took his place as judge" is a Greek phrase, which literally translated says, "sitting upon the bema."

THE REWARD SEAT

However, the bema seat was not only used to judge suspected criminals, it was also used as a place to present rewards. In the large Olympic arenas in the ancient world, there was an elevated seat on which the judge of the contest sat. After the contest was over, those who were successful in their competition would assemble before the bema to receive their rewards or crowns.

Therefore, in this instance, the bema was not a judicial bench where someone was condemned for their wrongdoings but rather it was a reward seat.

OUR SINS HAVE ALREADY BEEN JUDGED

Likewise, the Judgment Seat of Christ is not a judicial bench where believers are condemned for their sins. Our sins have been entirely paid for by Jesus Christ on the cross of Calvary. There is no more condemnation for those who are in Christ Jesus. The judgment of the sins of believers is a thing of the past.

Consequently, the Judgment Seat of Christ is actually the "Reward Seat." The Christian life is compared to a race which all believers run to win an eternal prize. Paul wrote.

> Don't you realize that in a race everyone runs, but only one person gets the prize? So run to win! All athletes are disciplined in their training. They do it to win a prize that will fade away, but we do it for an eternal prize. So I run with purpose in every step . . . (1 Corinthians 9:24-26 NLT).

Jesus Christ is the Judge or Rewarder of all Christians. After the race is over for each believer, He will gather every member before the His Judgment Seat, or bema, for the purpose of examining each one and giving the proper reward to each. The good news is that there is not merely one winner in the race which believers are running. Indeed, because we belong to Him, we are all winners and we all will be rewarded!

WHAT WILL HAPPEN AT THE JUDGMENT SEAT?

What will happen at this judgment seat of God? Who will be judged?

The Scriptures have the following to say.

1. ONLY NEW TESTAMENT BELIEVER'S WILL BE JUDGED (THE CHURCH)

The participants in the judgment seat of Christ, or the judgment seat of God, are members of the New Testament church. These are people who have trusted Jesus Christ as their Savior from the Day of Pentecost, when the church began, until the coming of Christ for His body or bride, the church. It does not include the Old Testament believers. They will have a separate time of judgment and reward.

Paul made it clear that this judgment is only for those have built their foundation on Jesus Christ. He wrote the following to the Corinthians.

> For no one can lay any other foundation than what has been laid down. That foundation is Jesus Christ . . . Each one's work will become obvious, for the day will disclose it, because it will be revealed by fire; the fire will test the quality of each one's work. If anyone's work that he has built survives, he will receive a reward. If anyone's work is burned up, it will be lost, but he will be saved; yet it will be like an escape through fire (1 Corinthians 3:11,13-15 HCSB).

Only believers receive rewards from God. Unbelievers, by definition, cannot do anything that pleases God. They will not receive any rewards, only condemnation.

2. IT WILL OCCUR BEFORE THE SECOND COMING OF CHRIST

The judging of New Testament believers will occur after the rapture of the church, but before the Second Coming of Christ to the earth.

In the Book of Revelation we read the following.

> Let us be glad, rejoice, and give Him glory, because the marriage of the Lamb has come, and His wife has prepared herself. She was given fine linen to wear, bright and pure. For the fine linen represents the righteous acts of the saints (Revelation 19:7,8 HCSB).

This is a picture of the believers before the Second Coming of Jesus Christ. We are told that the bride is clothed with righteous deeds. The church, therefore, has already been at the judgment seat of Christ because they are ready for the groom when He comes. Hence the judgment takes place sometime before the Second Coming of Christ.

3. THE RETURN OF THE LORD FOR HIS OWN: THE RAPTURE

The rapture of the church is the time that the Lord comes back for His own people. At some point in the future, known only to the Lord, Jesus Christ will return for those who have believed upon Him. The Lord will first resurrect the New Testament believers and then He will transform the bodies of those who are alive from corruptible to incorruptible. Paul explained this wonderful event when he wrote to the Thessalonians. He said.

> My friends, we want you to understand how it will be for those followers who have already died. Then you won't grieve over them and be like people who don't have any hope. We believe that Jesus died and was raised to life. We also believe that when God brings Jesus back again, he will bring with him all who had faith in Jesus before they died. Our Lord Jesus told us that when he comes, we won't go up to meet him ahead of his followers who have already died. With a loud command and with the shout of the chief angel and a blast of God's trumpet, the Lord will return from heaven. Then those who had faith in Christ before they died will be raised to life. Next, all of us who are still alive will be taken up into the clouds together with them to meet the Lord in the sky. From that time on we will all be with the Lord forever. Encourage each other with these words (1 Thessalonians 4:13-18 CEV).

After this event, all of those believers, those who have been raised as well as those who were taken up in the rapture, will go to the judgment seat of Christ. Judgment always comes *after* resurrection.

4. BELIEVERS ARE NOT JUDGED FOR THEIR SIN AT THE JUDGMENT SEAT

Again, it is important to realize that this is not a judgment to determine who will enter heaven. The sins of believers will not be an issue at the judgment seat of Christ. Indeed, they have already been forgiven once and for all. The Bible says.

> He doesn't punish us as our sins deserve. How great is God's love for all who worship him? Greater than the distance between heaven and earth! How far has the LORD taken our sins from us? Farther than the distance from east to west! (Psalm 103:10-12 CEV).

As far as the east is from the west so are our sins from us!

This is taught elsewhere. The prophet Micah wrote that they have been thrown into the depths of the ocean. He said.

> Once again you will have compassion on us. You will trample our sins under your feet and throw them into the depths of the ocean! (Micah 7:19 NLT).

Clearly, sin has already been judged. The judgment seat of Christ is for rewards.

THE DESTINY OF THE CHRISTIAN HAS BEEN SETTLED

With the death of Jesus Christ on the cross of Calvary, the destiny of the Christian has been once-and-for-all settled. There is no condemnation for those who have believed in Christ. Paul wrote.

> Therefore, no condemnation now exists for those in Christ Jesus (Romans 8:1 HCSB).

Those who have believed in Jesus will not be condemned. The penalty for our sins has already been paid for.

THEIR NAMES ARE WRITTEN IN THE BOOK OF LIFE

Believers in Christ are known as "overcomers. Those who overcome will have their names written in the Book of Life. Jesus said the following to the believers in the city of Sardis.

> Yet you have still a few names in Sardis, people who have not soiled their garments, and they will walk with me in white, for they are worthy. The one who conquers will be clothed thus in white garments, and I will never blot his name out of the book of life. I will confess his name before my Father and before his angels (Revelation 3:4,5 ESV).

Believers will be clothed in white garments, having their names written in the Book of Life. In addition, they will be acknowledged before God the Father and the holy angels.

BELIEVERS PRESENTLY HAVE ETERNAL LIFE

There is something else which is important for us to understand. The good news of the gospel is that those who have trusted Jesus Christ as their Savior presently possess eternal life. Jesus said.

> I assure you: Anyone who hears My word and believes Him who sent Me has eternal life and will not come under judgment but has passed from death to life (John 5:24 HCSB).

Eternal life is acquired the moment a person trusts Christ as his or her Savior. One a person believes in Jesus they enter into an eternal relationship with God the Father through God the Son. In other words, we possess eternal life right now!

THE CURSE HAS BEEN REMOVED BECAUSE OF JESUS

There is more good news! The Bible says that the curse against believers has been removed. Paul wrote to the Galatians.

> But Christ has rescued us from the curse pronounced by the law. When he was hung on the cross, he took upon himself the curse for our wrongdoing. For it is written in the Scriptures, "Cursed is everyone who is hung on a tree" (Galatians 3:13 NLT).

Jesus removed the curse for all of us by becoming a curse for us. His death upon the cross took the penalty for our sins.

THE PRICE HAS BEEN PAID FOR OUR SIN

The message of the New Testament is that Jesus Christ has paid the price for our sins. Peter wrote about this. He said.

> He himself bore our sins in his body on the cross, so that we might die to sins and live for righteousness; by his wounds you have been healed (1 Peter 2:24 NIV).

Since He has paid for our sins, we do not have to suffer for them. He has paid the price in full. There is nothing we can do to add to what He has done.

JESUS WAS A SIN OFFERING

At Calvary, He presented Himself as a sin offering on our behalf. Paul wrote the following to the Corinthians.

> For God made Christ, who never sinned, to be the offering for our sin, so that we could be made right with God through Christ (2 Corinthians 5:21 NLT).

The One who never sinned became an offering for sin. He died so that we could live. This is one of the great truths of Scripture.

Therefore, the believer's judgment, with respect to sin, is long past. Indeed, the Bible says that Jesus experienced death for everyone.

But we see Jesus, who was made a little lower than the angels, now crowned with glory and honor because he suffered death, so that by the grace of God he might taste death for everyone (Hebrews 2:9 NIV).

The main idea behind death is separation. He tasted death, or separation from God, for us so we do not have to personally experience it. On the cross, Jesus was spiritually separated from the Father when the penalty for the sins of the world was placed upon Him. Consequently, believers do not have to suffer for their own sins.

5. THE BELIEVERS WILL RECEIVE THEIR REWARDS AT THE JUDGMENT SEAT

Consequently, the judgment seat of Christ is not designed to punish believers, but rather to reward them for their faithful service. All of us will give an account of what we have done after trusting Christ as Savior.

Therefore, the judgment seat of Christ is a judgment of believer's works after salvation. Paul gave this analogy.

According to the grace of God given to me, like a skilled master builder I laid a foundation, and someone else is building upon it. Let each one take care how he builds upon it. For no one can lay a foundation other than that which is laid, which is Jesus Christ. Now if anyone builds on the foundation with gold, silver, precious stones, wood, hay, straw— each one's work will become manifest, for the Day will disclose it, because it will be revealed by fire, and the fire will test what sort of work each one has done (1 Corinthians 3:10-13 ESV).

Therefore, the works performed after a person becomes a Christian will be examined. The good works will be separated from the bad. Rewards will be given for these good works.

ALL OF OUR ACTIONS WILL BE EXAMINED

The Bible says that God will reward the actions of believers. The psalmist wrote about the Lord rewarding His people.

> And that you, O Lord, are loving. Surely you will reward each person according to what he has done (Psalm 62:12 NIV).

God has promised to reward those who trust in Him. The rewards will be based upon our actions as believers in Christ.

The Apostle Paul wrote about the rewards of the Lord. He said the following to the Ephesians about what we will receive for the good which we do.

> Serve with a good attitude, as to the Lord and not to men, knowing that whatever good each one does, slave or free, he will receive this back from the Lord (Ephesians 6:7,8 HCSB).

Every single thing we have done will be evaluated and the good will be rewarded.

HE KNOWS WHAT MOTIVATES US

The Lord will not only judged our deeds, He will also judge what motivates us. Paul wrote.

> So don't judge anyone until the Lord returns. He will show what is hidden in the dark and what is in everyone's heart. Then God will be the one who praises each of us (1 Corinthians 4:5 CEV).

So it is not just a matter of what we do, it is also a matter of what motivates us to do it. Indeed, He knows what is in our heart.

OUR WORKS WILL BE TESTED BY FIRE

The judgment will be by means of fire. Paul wrote to the Corinthians.

The day will make what each one does clearly visible because fire will reveal it. That fire will determine what kind of work each person has done. If what a person has built survives, he will receive a reward. If his work is burned up, he will suffer the loss. However, he will be saved, though it will be like going through a fire (1 Corinthians 3:13-14 God's Word).

Fire is often used in Scripture as a symbol of judgment. The Bible describes the glorified Christ in this manner.

The hairs of his head were white, like white wool, like snow. His eyes were like a flame of fire (Revelation 1:14 ESV).

His eyes of fire represent eyes that will judge.

In another place, the Lord is described as a consuming fire. Moses wrote that the Lord is a jealous God who will punish sin.

For the LORD your God is a consuming fire, a jealous God (Deuteronomy 4:24 NIV).

Fire will purify the works of the believer.

6. SOME WILL SUFFER LOSS OF THEIR REWARD

Not everyone will receive the same reward when believers are gathered together for evaluation. Indeed, we are told that at the judgment seat of Jesus Christ, there will be those who suffer loss.

Paul made this clear to the Corinthians. He said.

If his work is burned up, he will suffer the loss. However, he will be saved, though it will be like going through a fire (1 Corinthians 3:13-15 God's Word).

Some people will lose their heavenly reward. Again, they will not lose heaven itself, merely the reward in heaven.

Paul wrote elsewhere about suffering loss as a believer in Christ. In writing to the Corinthians he made the following comparison.

> Do you not know that in a race all the runners run, but only one receives the prize? So run that you may obtain it. Every athlete exercises self-control in all things. They do it to receive a perishable wreath, but we an imperishable. So I do not run aimlessly; I do not box as one beating the air. But I discipline my body and keep it under control, lest after preaching to others I myself should be disqualified (1 Corinthians 9:24-27 ESV).

Paul gave the analogy of running a race. He did not want to be disqualified from the race. Indeed, he wanted to win. Consequently he practiced self-control.

We emphasize that the idea of being disqualified has nothing to do with the loss of salvation; Paul was concerned with the loss of reward. His salvation was eternally secure.

WE MUST BE CAREFUL NOT TO LOSE OUR REWARD

Scripture elsewhere warns believers about losing their reward. In the Book of Revelation we find Jesus saying the following to believers.

> I am coming soon! Hold on to what you have so that no one takes your crown (Revelation 3:11 God's Word).

It is possible to lose the reward or the crown which symbolizes the reward.

AN ILLUSTRATION OF THE LOSS OF REWARD

We can illustrate the loss of reward in the following manner: Let us say you have recently built a new two-story house. While on the second floor, you smell smoke. Looking downstairs you see that the first floor is on fire. You jump out the second story window to save your life. You then watch your new house burn to the ground.

Obviously you will have mixed emotions. You're thankful that you were able to jump and save your life, but you are sad because your new house is destroyed. This is similar to those believers who are saved but have nothing to show for it. They squandered their opportunities to live for Christ yet they are enjoying the benefits of heaven with Jesus.

BELIEVERS WILL WANT TO APPEAR WITHOUT SHAME BEFORE CHRIST

Indeed, it is actually possible that believers will appear before this judgment seat of God and be ashamed. John wrote.

> Now, dear children, live in Christ. Then, when he appears we
> will have confidence, and when he comes we won't turn from
> him in shame (1 John 2:28 God's Word).

Consequently, our goal should be to appear without shame when we come face to face with Jesus Christ as our Judge or Rewarder.

Indeed, we want to be confident, not fearful, in the Day of Judgment. We do not want to be frightened of losing our reward. Whether we will be ashamed or not is completely up to us. Our behavior as Christians in this life will determine whether or not we will be ashamed on that day.

THE REWARDS WILL BE OF OUR OWN MAKING

To sum up, the rewards we receive in heaven will be of our own making. While salvation is a free gift, rewards are earned. In fact, the Bible says that the wise will shine. We read in Daniel.

> Those who are wise will shine like the brightness of the heavens, and those who lead many to righteousness, like the stars for ever and ever (Daniel 12:3 NIV).

Our garments will shine but they will not all shine the same. While every believer is at the Wedding Feast of Christ and dressed in white garments, we will not all be dressed the same or rewarded the same. It will depend upon how faithful we have been to the ministry the Lord has given to each of us. Therefore, today each of us is making our own garments for that day of reward.

SOME PEOPLE HAVE A DIFFERENT VIEW OF THE JUDGMENT SEAT OF CHRIST

We must note that not all Christians believe the judgment seat of Christ will be limited to New Testament believers. Many Christians hold the view that this is part of one general judgment of all humanity; not a number of separate judgments. They believe that the Bible teaches that all humanity, not just New Testament Christians, will be judged at the same time. They equate this judgment with the judgment of the nations spoken of in Matthew 25:31-46 and the Great White Throne Judgment in Revelation 20:10-15.

There are two views as to when this general judgment of humanity will occur. One view sees it occurring at the Second Coming of Christ while another viewpoint has it happening at the end of a thousand year period of the rule of Christ upon the earth, the Millennium.

THE BASIC QUESTION: IS THERE AN INTERMEDIATE EARTHLY KINGDOM?

As we have noted, there is a basic question regarding the future to which Bible believers have a difference of opinion. Simply stated, it is this: Is there an intermediate earthly kingdom when the Lord Jesus returns, a Millennium, or does His eternal kingdom begin at the Second Coming of Christ. In other words, does the end to history, as we know it, consist of an intermediate one thousand year earthly kingdom followed by eternity or does eternity begin immediately with the Second Coming of Jesus Christ? This is the question on which good Christians differ.

However, though there is disagreement on the timing of the judgment seat of Christ, as well whether or not there is an intermediate earthly kingdom before the eternal realm, there is no disagreement that this judgment for the believer will be a day of reward.

Again we emphasize that for the Christian "Judgment Day" is "Reward Day." Indeed, it is not a judgment to determine whether certain people will enter heaven, but rather it is a judgment that decides to what extent God will reward those who will spend eternity with Him.

SUMMARY TO QUESTION 28
HOW WILL BELIEVER'S BE JUDGED?
(THE JUDGMENT SEAT OF CHRIST: THE BEMA)

The Bible speaks of a future event called the judgment seat of Christ. It is a time of examination and reward for New Testament believers in Jesus. The Old Testament saints will not be judged at this time, it is limited to New Testament believers.

For this time of evaluation, the Lord will resurrect the bodies of the saints who have died during the church age. He will also change the bodies of those still alive as He takes them up into heaven in an event called the rapture. They will be given a glorified body without having to die. All believers will meet the Lord in the air and proceed to the judgment seat of Christ.

This judgment will consist of rewards for faithful service. There will be no condemning of anyone. Indeed, there is no condemnation for those who believe in Jesus Christ. Instead, there will be degrees of reward given to believers.

Some will receive greater rewards than others. The rewards will be proportionate to our faithfulness. Our ultimate desire, therefore, should be to please the Lord as we look forward to this time of reward.

We are also told that some will be ashamed at that time and lose their reward. This pictures believers in Christ who have squandered the gifts He has given to them. Their lives will be characterized by self rather than by Christ. This fact should encourage each and every one of us who have believed in Jesus to live our lives in such a way that we will not be ashamed at His coming. Indeed, we want to look forward to that day.

It is important to note that not all Christians see the judgment seat of Christ as a separate judgment for believers only. They think it is part of one general judgment for all humanity on one particular day. This judgment will take place either at the Second Coming of Christ or at the end of the Millennium, the thousand year reign of Christ upon the earth.

Whatever differences Christians may have with respect to the timing of these judgments, believers are in agreement as to what is going to happen. Those who have trusted Jesus Christ will be brought before Him to receive their rewards for faithful service. They will not be condemned.

Again, we cannot stress the fact too strongly that there is no condemnation for those who have trusted Jesus Christ as Savior.

What Things Should We Do In This Life To Earn Rewards In The Next Life? (On What Basis, Or Criteria, Will Believers We Be Judged)

According to the Bible, Christians are people who have believed in Jesus Christ as their Savior. They are saved from their sins by putting their trust in Him. It has nothing to do with their own good works. Salvation is entirely a work of God. Paul explained it this way.

> God saved you through faith as an act of kindness. You had nothing to do with it. Being saved is a gift from God. It's not the result of anything you've done, so no one can brag about it (Ephesians 2:8,9 God's Word).

We cannot earn our salvation. It is a free gift which is offered to us by God the Father through His Son Jesus Christ. We receive it by placing our faith in Jesus.

In addition, those who believe in Him are said to be "in Christ." The Bible says that there is no condemnation for those who are "in Christ." Paul wrote.

> There is therefore now no condemnation for those who are in Christ Jesus (Romans 8:1 NET).

Because we have believed in Jesus Christ we will not have to pay for our own sins. Jesus took the punishment for us. No condemnation awaits believers. None whatsoever!

THERE IS A REWARD DAY FOR BELIEVERS

There will, however, come a judgment day for Christians. This judgment does not consist of condemnation but of rewards. These rewards will be based upon our actions *after* we have believed in Jesus. We are not saved by our good works but our works will earn us rewards.

Therefore, judgment day for the believer is "reward day." On that day we want to hear the following words from Jesus.

Well done, good and faithful servant (Matthew 25:21 NIV).

This brings up a number of questions. On what basis will believers be rewarded? What are the criteria that the Lord has set down? In other words, what can we do in this life to earn rewards in the next? Specifically, what things should we do in order to hear the words "well done" from Jesus?

WE MUST UNDERSTAND THAT EARNING REWARDS IS NOT SELFISH

Before we look at some of the criteria the Lord has set down, we must first deal with a question that often arises, "Isn't seeking rewards selfish?" In other words, why should we worry about what type of crowns or rewards we will receive in the next life? Aren't we going to cast our crowns, or rewards, at the feet of Jesus? Shouldn't we merely seek to love and serve Christ? Isn't that enough?

These type of questions reveal a misunderstanding of what the Bible teaches about the rewards which will be given to the believer. In fact, rewards are the evaluation of our life from God's perspective. In other words, they are given to Christians for faithful service to the Lord. Therefore, rewards are based upon how obedient we have been to Him in this life. Hence, seeking rewards should be seen as "seeking to please the Lord." In sum, the rewards are the result of our obedient behavior.

WHAT WILL OUR REWARDS BE BASED UPON?

The Bible says that our heavenly reward will be based upon a number of things. They are as follows.

CRITERION NUMBER ONE: HOW WELL WE RUN THE RACE

The Apostle Paul compared the Christian life to running a race. The overall reward we will receive will depend upon how well we have run the race of life. Paul wrote the following to the church in Corinth.

> Do you not know that in a race all the runners run, but only one gets the prize? Run in such a way as to get the prize. Everyone who competes in the games goes into strict training. They do it to get a crown that will not last; but we do it to get a crown that will last forever. Therefore I do not run like a man running aimlessly; I do not fight like a man beating the air. No, I beat my body and make it my slave so that after I have preached to others, I myself will not be disqualified for the prize (1 Corinthians 9:24-27 NIV).

It must be emphasized that in this race we are not competing against one another. Indeed, we are only competing against ourselves. He will reward us based upon how we have acted after our conversion to Christ.

RUNNING THE RACE WITH ETERNITY IN VIEW

We run the race of life with eternity in view. This is our finish line. Our goal, therefore, should be to keep our eye on the prize. Paul wrote to the Philippians.

> It's not that I've already reached the goal or have already completed the course. But I run to win that which Jesus Christ has already won for me. Brothers and sisters, I can't consider myself a winner yet. This is what I do: I don't look back, I lengthen my stride, and I run straight toward the goal to win the prize that God's heavenly call offers in Christ Jesus. Whoever has a mature faith should think this way (Philippians 3:12-15 God's Word).

Paul emphasized that we must put our past experiences behind us as we run the race of life. Indeed, our eyes should always be looking ahead to our ultimate goal, eternity with the Lord in heaven. In other words, we are never to look back, we are only to keep moving forward. The past must remain in the past.

THE RACE OF LIFE IS A BATTLE: WE WEAR ARMOR

There is something else we need to understand about this race of life; it is a battle, a struggle. In fact it is more like running a gauntlet.

Indeed, we have enemies, spiritual powers, that are attempting to keep us from succeeding. Therefore, we need to run the race wearing the armor of God. This was made clear by Paul in his letter to the Ephesians.

> We are not fighting against humans. We are fighting against forces and authorities and against rulers of darkness and powers in the spiritual world. So put on all the armor that God gives. Then when that evil day comes, you will be able to defend yourself. And when the battle is over, you will still be standing firm (Ephesians 6:12-13 CEV).

Therefore, with our eyes upon the finish line, eternity, we run the race of life wearing the armor of God. If we do this, then we will be well on our way to hearing those words, "well done, good and faithful servant."

CRITERION NUMBER TWO: HOW FAITHFUL WE ARE TO OUR CALLING

Above all, in this race, God has called us to be faithful. Paul wrote about how believers ought to be thought of by others.

> People should think of us as servants of Christ and managers who are entrusted with God's mysteries. Managers are required to be trustworthy (1 Corinthians 4:1-2 God's Word).

The main requirement that the Lord expects from believers is trustworthiness. He wants us to be faithful with the various gifts which He has given to us.

THE PURPOSE OF OUR GIFTS: TO SERVE OTHERS

Ultimately, this is the key. We are to be found faithful with the things which God has given to us. The goal is to serve others.

Indeed, if we could sum up the life and ministry of Jesus Christ in one word it would be the word "others." In fact, the Bible explains the purpose of Jesus' coming to earth in this manner.

> It's the same way with the Son of Man. He didn't come so that others could serve him. He came to serve and to give his life as a ransom for many people (Matthew 20:28 God's Word).

Therefore, we are to manage the gifts which the Lord has given to us so that we can be a benefit to others.

THERE ARE DIFFERENT DEGREES OF REWARDS

Jesus Himself spoke of different degrees of rewards in one of the parables that He gave. We read of this in Luke's gospel where our Lord told the following story about a man who entrusted his goods to his slave.

> The king said to him, 'Good job! You're a good servant. You proved that you could be trusted with a little money. Take charge of ten cities.' "The second servant said, 'The coin you gave me, sir, has made five times as much.' "The king said to this servant, 'You take charge of five cities (Luke 19:17-19 God's Word).

One man was to rule ten cities while another five cities. Therefore we find there are degrees of rewards based upon our faithfulness.

Thus, the rewards that the believer receives in the next life will be proportionate to the faithfulness they show in this life.

In sum, faithfulness is the key. This is what the Lord is looking for in those who belong to Him.

Consequently, we must be faithful to the tasks which He has given to us. This will be the basis for the eternal rewards for those who believe in Jesus Christ.

CRITERION NUMBER THREE: HOW WE ENDURE PERSECUTION

As we run the race of life, there is something else we must also realize. Those who believe in Jesus Christ, will, at times, be persecuted. This is especially true if we desire to live a godly life. Paul wrote.

> In fact, all those who want to live a godly life in Christ Jesus will be persecuted (2 Timothy 3:12 HCSB).

The Contemporary English Version puts it this way.

> Anyone who belongs to Christ Jesus and wants to live right will have trouble from others (2 Timothy 3:12 CEV).

Trouble will indeed come from others when we live a godly life.

In fact, Jesus also made it clear that persecution will be part of the experience of the Christian who desires to follow Him. In the Sermon on the Mount, He said the following.

> Blessed are you when people insult you, persecute you and falsely say all kinds of evil against you because of me. Rejoice and be glad, because great is your reward in heaven, for in the same way they persecuted the prophets who were before you (Matthew 5:11-12 NIV).

According to Jesus, we will be eternally rewarded based upon how we deal with the persecution we receive from others.

CRITERION NUMBER FOUR: HOW WE ENDURE SUFFERING

Life is difficult for every human being. Indeed, we find that even Christians are not promised that everything will be easy for them in this life. There is no guarantee that we will escape suffering and hardships. Indeed, the Bible assumes we will suffer. Peter wrote the following to his fellow believers.

> Dear friends, don't be surprised or shocked that you are going through testing that is like walking through fire (1 Peter 4:12 CEV).

We should not be surprised if we are tested. In fact, testing is a normal part of our Christian experience.

James said that our reward in heaven will be based upon how well we have endured suffering. He put it this way.

> Blessed are those who endure when they are tested. When they pass the test, they will receive the crown of life that God has promised to those who love him (James 1:12 God's Word).

We will be tested, we will suffer. There is no doubt about it. Therefore, another basis for our everlasting reward in heaven is our response to the suffering which we will experience here upon the earth.

CRITERION NUMBER FIVE: HOW WE GET THE MESSAGE OF CHRIST TO THE LOST

An additional part of our heavenly reward will be determined by our fervor to get God's Word to those who are lost. People are either saved or they are lost. This includes every human being. Indeed, there is no in-between state. If they are lost, then they need to be saved. Christians have the *only* message which can save them.

Indeed, Jesus made this clear. We read His words.

> For this reason I told you that you'll die because of your sins. If you don't believe that I am the one, you'll die because of your sins (John 8:24 God's Word).

There is no hope without Jesus. This is what He claimed!

THE ILLUSTRATION FROM THE LIFE OF PAUL

For example, the Apostle Paul said his prize or reward in God's presence will be the people he taught, as well as those whom he brought to faith in Jesus Christ. He wrote the following to the Thessalonians.

> Who is our hope, joy, or prize that we can brag about in the presence of our Lord Jesus when he comes? Isn't it you? You are our glory and joy! (1 Thessalonians 2:19-20 God's Word).

Like Paul, the desire of each of us should be to reach the lost with the good news of Jesus Christ. We will be rewarded based upon how well we spread the gospel of Christ during our time here upon the earth.

CRITERION NUMBER SIX: HOW WE TREAT FELLOW-BELIEVERS

Part of our future reward will be based upon how we treat our fellow-believers in Jesus. In fact, the Lord said that people will know we are Christians by the love which we have for one another.

On the night of Jesus' betrayal, John records Him saying the following to His disciples.

> I'm giving you a new commandment: Love each other in the same way that I have loved you. Everyone will know that you are my disciples because of your love for each other (John 13:34,35 God's Word).

The mark of the Christian is the love they show one to another. Indeed, this is how others will know that we are His followers.

The writer to the Hebrews emphasized that our reward will be based upon how we have helped our fellow-believers. We read the following words.

> God is not unjust; he will not forget your work and the love you have shown him as you have helped his people and continue to help them (Hebrews 6:10 NIV).

The treatment of fellow Christians, those who have believed in Jesus, will be one of the factors for our heavenly reward.

CRITERION NUMBER SEVEN: HOW WE TREAT STRANGERS AND THE LESS FORTUNATE

Christians are supposed to reach out to those who are the less fortunate. This includes people whom we do not personally know. Jesus said that our treatment of the poor, and of strangers, will be rewarded on that day when we see Him face to face. Luke wrote.

> Then Jesus said to the man who had invited him: When you give a dinner or a banquet, don't invite your friends and family and relatives and rich neighbors. If you do, they will invite you in return, and you will be paid back. When you give a feast, invite the poor, the crippled, the lame, and the blind. They cannot pay you back. But God will bless you and reward you when his people rise from death (Luke 14:12-14 CEV).

In reaching the world for Jesus Christ, we need to remember to reach out to the poor and the needy. We should not merely spend time with our friends, family, and rich neighbors. There are others who need our help. Our heavenly reward will be based upon how faithful we are to this commandment.

CRITERION NUMBER EIGHT: HOW WE CONTROL THE WORDS WHICH COME OUT OF OUR MOUTHS

Scripture emphasizes that believers in Jesus are to control what comes out of their mouths. In fact, this is what Jesus Himself said. We read the following words of our Lord.

> But I tell you that men will have to give account on the day of judgment for every careless word they have spoken (Matthew 12:36 NIV).

We must be careful what we say.

The New Testament writer James wrote about the necessity of controlling what comes out of our mouths. He put it this way.

> Dear brothers and sisters, not many of you should become teachers in the church, for we who teach will be judged by God with greater strictness. We all make many mistakes, but those who control their tongues can also control themselves in every other way (James 3:1-2 NLT).

Our speech needs to be under control. Therefore, our own words will determine the degree of reward we will receive in the afterlife.

CRITERION NUMBER NINE: HOW WE USE OUR MONEY

There is a very practical way by which we can show our devotion to Jesus; how we use our money. Indeed, a person who believes in Jesus Christ can demonstrate their love for him by the proper use of their money.

Jesus Himself emphasized this. In the Sermon on the Mount He said.

> Be careful not to do your good works in public in order to attract attention. If you do, your Father in heaven will not reward you. So when you give to the poor, don't announce it with trumpet fanfare. This is what hypocrites do in the synagogues and on the streets in order to be praised by people. I can guarantee this truth: That will be their only reward. When you give to the poor, don't let your left hand know what your right hand is doing. Give your contributions privately. Your Father sees what you do in private. He will reward you (Matthew 6:1-4 God's Word).

If we do love the Lord, then we will use our money to further His kingdom. While we are to contribute financially to the kingdom of God but we are commanded to do it privately. We should not seek after any glory for the gifts which we give.

Paul wrote to Timothy about the proper use of riches. He gave him some very practical advice as to what to tell others who are rich.

> Tell those who have the riches of this world not to be arrogant and not to place their confidence in anything as uncertain as riches. Instead, they should place their confidence in God who richly provides us with everything to enjoy. Tell them to do good, to do a lot of good things, to be generous, and to share. By doing this they store up a treasure for themselves which is a good foundation for the future. In this way they take hold of what life really is (1 Timothy 6:17-19 God's Word).

The use or misuse of the money the Lord has provided to us will help determine our heavenly reward. Indeed, we show our true feelings by how we spend our money.

Jesus summed up the issue of the believer and money in the following manner.

> Do not store up for yourselves treasures on earth, where moths and vermin destroy, and where thieves break in and steal. But store up for yourselves treasures in heaven, where moths and vermin do not destroy, and where thieves do not break in and steal. For where your treasure is, there your heart will be also (Matthew 6:19-21 NIV).

This should cause us to ask ourselves the question: where are we storing up our treasures?

CRITERION NUMBER TEN: HOW MUCH WE ARE LOOKING FORWARD TO THE RETURN OF CHRIST

Finally, our future reward will be based upon our attitude concerning the return of Jesus Christ.

The Apostle Paul wrote to Timothy about his attitude toward the coming of Christ.

My life is coming to an end, and it is now time for me to be poured out as a sacrifice to God. I have fought the good fight. I have completed the race. I have kept the faith. The prize that shows I have God's approval is now waiting for me. The Lord, who is a fair judge, will give me that prize on that day. He will give it not only to me but also to everyone who is eagerly waiting for him to come again (2 Timothy 4:6-8 God's Word).

Paul was looking forward to the time of Christ's return. Among other things, there was a prize waiting for him, as there will be for the rest of us, who are eagerly anticipating the Lord's coming.

Indeed, our desire should be for the return of Jesus Christ. To the degree we are looking forward to His return is another factor which will determine our reward.

HOW SHOULD WE THEN LIVE?

These are merely some of the factors which will determine the rewards that believers will receive at the judgment seat of Christ. We should be constantly keeping these things in mind as we live our lives in anticipation of His return.

In addition, there are two very practical aspects about understanding what Scripture says about the basis of our future rewards as believers. They are as follows.

UNDERSTANDING THE FUTURE REWARDS SHOULD MOTIVATE US TO LIVE GODLY

The fact that Jesus Christ will reward us should inspire us to live a godly life. Paul said that his desire was to please Him. Paul wrote.

So whether we are at home or away, we make it our aim to please him (2 Corinthians 5:9 ESV).

We should desire that our life is pleasing to Him. This should be our ultimate goal.

IT SHOULD MAKE US WANT TO ENCOURAGE ONE ANOTHER

The fact that the Lord will reward those who serve Him should cause believers to encourage one another. The writer to the Hebrews said.

> We should keep on encouraging each other to be thoughtful and to do helpful things. Some people have gotten out of the habit of meeting for worship, but we must not do that. We should keep on encouraging each other, especially since you know that the day of the Lord's coming is getting closer (Hebrews 10:24,25 CEV).

As we get closer to the time of the end, we are to be encouragers of one another. This is what pleases the Lord.

In sum, "Reward Day" is indeed coming for all believers in Jesus. As we live out our lives, may we always keep this thought in the forefront of our minds!

SUMMARY TO QUESTION 29
WHAT THINGS SHOULD WE DO IN THIS LIFE TO EARN REWARDS IN THE NEXT LIFE? (ON WHAT BASIS, OR CRITERIA, WILL BELIEVERS BE JUDGED)

The Bible says that everyone will be judged but not everyone will be judged the same way. Indeed, unbelievers will be condemned at the Last Judgment for their lack of belief in Jesus. No matter how "good" they may have been in this life, it will not matter at the final judgment. They are not good enough. In fact, unless they receive Jesus Christ as their Savior, they are forever lost. Without Christ there is no hope.

On the other hand, believers in Christ will receive no condemnation. Christ has taken the penalty of our sins upon Himself. Therefore, believers will receive rewards. This will occur at the judgment seat of Christ.

In addition, Scripture tells us what our rewards will be based upon. Indeed, the Lord has given us the criteria, or the standards, as to how He will evaluate us. This includes the following.

To begin with, the overall rewards will be based upon how we run the race of life. Ultimately, the degree to which we are rewarded is the degree we are faithful to our calling. Our rewards will be based upon our faithfulness. This is crucial to realize.

The Bible says that believers will be persecuted. How we respond to persecution will be a basis for our rewards.

Believers will also suffer in this life. Our rewards will be also be given to us based upon the way we respond to suffering.

It is important that we reach the lost with the message of Jesus Christ. To the extent which we do it will determine our heavenly reward. Indeed, we are left here upon the earth to reach out to others with the message of Christ.

Jesus will also reward each of us based upon how we treat our fellow believers. In fact, He said that people will know we are His followers by the love which we express one to another. This is the mark of the Christian.

The treatment of strangers will also be used to determine our heavenly reward. The Bible says we are to reach out to the poor and needy and extend a helping hand. We are to help those who cannot help us and cannot pay us back for our help. The Lord will be the One who rewards us for this.

How we use the money God entrusted us will also be a basis for our reward. The Lord has entrusted a certain amount of worldly riches to each of us. We are to use them wisely. Our reward will be based upon how we use the resources the Lord has entrusted to us.

Finally, the way in which we look forward to the return of Jesus Christ will also determine our reward. Do we long for His appearing? Is His return something which motives our behavior? It should. Our reward will be based, in part, to the degree we are looking for Him to come back and set up His kingdom.

These are some of the ways in which the Lord will determine the reward in heaven. Consequently, we should take seriously these things He has told us and live our lives accordingly.

Will Every Believer In Jesus Christ Receive A Reward In Heaven?

Believers in Jesus Christ are to be rewarded on judgment day, they are not condemned. Indeed, for those who trust Christ judgment day is actually "reward day." All of us will appear before Him to receive rewards for what we have done since the time we believed in Him.

This brings up a question. Will every believer receive a reward on that day or will there be those who will have basically nothing to receive because they have squandered the gifts the Lord has given to them?

THE CASE FOR EVERY BELIEVER RECEIVING A REWARD

Many Christians assume that each believer will receive some type of reward at the judgment seat of Christ. This is usually assumed from the following statement of Paul.

> Therefore don't judge anything prematurely, before the Lord comes, who will both bring to light what is hidden in darkness and reveal the intentions of the hearts. And then praise will come to each one from God (1 Corinthians 4:5 HCSB).

Paul says praise will come to each person from the Lord. This seemingly makes it clear that each believer will receive some type of praise from the Lord.

We are also told that every believer will rule with Christ in His coming kingdom. In his last letter before his death, Paul wrote the following to Timothy.

> If we endure, we will also reign with him. If we disown him, he will also disown us (2 Timothy 2:12 NIV).

This further indicates that every believer will receive a reward on judgment day as well as praise from the Lord for faithful service. In sum, everyone will indeed receive praise and rewards.

THE CASE FOR EVERY BELIEVER NOT NECESSARILY RECEIVING A REWARD

There are those who are not convinced that everyone at the judgment seat of Christ will receive a reward. They do not believe that this will necessarily be the case. While this is a place where believers will be rewarded, it is not certain that everyone will receive a reward.

Paul says that at the judgment seat of Christ, the Lord will bring to light "the hidden things of darkness and reveal the true motives of our heart." While this will not result in condemnation for the believer, it will result in exposing our genuine motives. Though our sins have been forgiven, and will not be held against us, our motives will be made known. This includes our bad motives. We will only be rewarded for things done with the proper motive.

This is important to understand. We will not merely be rewarded for what we do; we will be rewarded based upon the motivation behind these deeds. There will be shame and rebuke for those deeds which we did with the wrong motives. John wrote about this.

> So now, little children, remain in Him, so that when He appears we may have boldness and not be ashamed before Him at His coming (1 John 2:28 HCSB).

We certainly do not want to have any shame when the Lord judges us. Realizing this should impact the way we conduct our lives. We want to appear before the Lord without shame and without being rebuked for wrong motives. Since these are real possibilities we need to examine why we do what we do.

PAUL DOES NOT SAY EVERYONE WILL BE PRAISED

Furthermore, it is argued that Paul does not clearly say that everyone would have his or her worked praised on the day of rewards. Rather he said that the "faithful" work of everyone will be praised. He did not intend to say that the "work" of everyone will be praised.

Indeed, he was not saying that everything we do will be praised since he made it clear the motives of each of us would be examined. To please the Lord at the judgment seat of Christ, we must be faithful with the gifts which He has given to us, as well as having the correct motives in using these gifts.

In fact, a Christian can do the right things with the wrong motives. While each believer will rule with Christ in His kingdom, the rulership will be greater for those whose motives were godly. They will receive praise from the Lord as well as a greater reward.

Again, we stress the key is obedience. We should obey the commandments of the Lord but we should always do it with the right motive. As Jesus said, if we love Him then we will indeed keep His commandments.

SUMMARY TO QUESTION 30
WILL EVERY BELIEVER IN JESUS CHRIST RECEIVE A REWARD IN HEAVEN?

There is a question among Bible-believers as to whether or not each person who appears before the judgment seat of Jesus Christ will receive a reward. Punishment for sin is not an issue since the judgment seat of Christ is where rewards are handed out and believers receive praise for their deeds done after they have trusted Christ.

Many people think the Bible teaches that every believer will receive some sort of reward as well as a certain degree of praise at the judgment seat of

Christ. Everyone who appears before the judgment seat, or the reward seat, will receive something for his or her efforts here upon the earth.

However, others disagree. They believe that it is possible for a believer to be part of the kingdom of Christ, to rule and reign with Him, but not to receive any reward or praise on the Day of Judgment.

The reason this position is held is because the Scripture speaks of examining the motives behind our actions to determine whether they are good or bad. This assumes some of our motives are not pure.

Furthermore, John said that it was possible for believers to be ashamed when Christ returned. This speaks of loss of reward. It seems that we can be ashamed to some degree when we stand before Christ because we have wasted the opportunities which have been afforded to us.

All of this should encourage one another to examine ourselves and the work we do for the Lord. Are we doing it with the proper motives? Are we seeking His glory and not ours? These issues need to be taken seriously for there will come a day when our deeds, as well as our motives, will be accurately revealed.

Whom Will Christ Judge At His Second Coming? (The Judgment Of The Nations)

When Jesus Christ returns to the earth at His Second Coming, He will return in judgment. Jesus Himself spoke of this coming judgment as He concluded His last discourse to His disciples. His words are recorded in Matthew 25:31-46. They read, in part, as follows.

> When the Son of Man comes in his glory, and all the angels with him, then he will sit on his glorious throne. Before him will be gathered all the nations, and he will separate people one from another as a shepherd separates the sheep from the goats. And he will place the sheep on his right, but the goats on the left. Then the King will say to those on his right, 'Come, you who are blessed by my Father, inherit the kingdom prepared for you from the foundation of the world.' . . . Then he will say to those on his left, 'Depart from me, you cursed, into the eternal fire prepared for the devil and his angels. And these will go away into eternal punishment, but the righteous into eternal life (Matthew 25:31-34,41,46 ESV).

The kingdom awaits the righteous while punishment is the destiny of the unbeliever.

The Apostle Paul also taught this truth; Jesus will judge humanity when He returns. He wrote the following words to the Thessalonians.

And God will provide rest for you who are being persecuted and also for us when the Lord Jesus appears from heaven. He will come with his mighty angels, in flaming fire, bringing judgment on those who don't know God and on those who refuse to obey the Good News of our Lord Jesus. They will be punished with everlasting destruction, forever separated from the Lord and from his glorious power (2 Thessalonians 1:7-9 NLT).

The Second Coming of Jesus Christ will be a time of relief or rest for believers and vengeance for unbelievers. Scripture makes this clear.

This brings up a number of important issues. Whom will Jesus Christ judge when He returns to the earth? Who will enter His promised kingdom?

THE PREMILLENNIAL VIEW OF THE FUTURE

We will answer this question according to the premillennial view of "things to come." After stating the premillennial view, we will summarize other views of these judgments. Put simply, the premillennial view is as follows.

There will be a literal one thousand-year reign of Jesus Christ upon the earth after His Second Coming to our world. Therefore, we find that Jesus returns to earth, pre, or before, that thousand year reign, the Millennium, begins. Millennium is the Latin word for thousand.

In other words, the return of Christ to the earth does not begin the eternal state for humanity. Instead there will be an intermediate earthly kingdom that will last a thousand years. During this interval Jesus will rule and reign upon the earth. After the thousand years is over then the eternal state will begin.

HE WILL RULE FROM JERUSALEM

When Jesus does return, He will fulfill a number of specific promises contained in the Old Testament. For example, Jesus, as the Messiah, will set up an earthly kingdom where He will rule from the city of Jerusalem.

We read the following in the Book of Isaiah.

> This is what Isaiah son of Amoz saw concerning Judah and Jerusalem: In the last days the mountain of the Lord's temple will be established as the highest of the mountains; it will be exalted above the hills, and all nations will stream to it. Many peoples will come and say, "Come, let us go up to the mountain of the Lord, to the temple of the God of Jacob. He will teach us his ways, so that we may walk in his paths." The law will go out from Zion, the word of the Lord from Jerusalem. He will judge between the nations and will settle disputes for many peoples. They will beat their swords into plowshares and their spears into pruning hooks. Nation will not take up sword against nation, nor will they train for war anymore (Isaiah 2:1-5 NIV).

This is similar to a number of promises made to the nation of Israel. He will rule in righteousness for one thousand years with Jerusalem as His headquarters.

THE LAST JUDGMENT

At the end of this thousand-year reign of the Messiah, there will be the Last Judgment. At that time, all the unbelieving dead who have ever lived will be judged.

After this event occurs, the Lord will create a new heaven and new earth. This will be inhabited by believers only. For all eternity, believers will enjoy the wonder of His presence! This sums up the premillennial view of future events.

WHO WILL BE JUDGED WHEN CHRIST RETURNS ACCORDING TO THE PREMILLENNIAL VIEW?

According to the premillennial view, there will be four separate groups of people whom the Lord will judge when He returns to the earth.

1. Those Living From The Nation Israel

2. The Gentile Nations

3. The Old Testament Saints

4. The Tribulation Saints

The church, the body of Christ, will have already been judged and rewarded before Jesus returns to the earth. This takes place at the judgment seat of Christ, also called the judgment seat of God. These believers will return with Christ at His Second Coming and will rule and reign with Him during His earthly kingdom and beyond.

The Bible has the following to say about those who will be judged at His Second Coming.

GROUP 1: THE LIVING FROM ISRAEL

When Jesus Christ returns to the earth in triumph, He will judge those from the nation of Israel who have survived the Great Tribulation. This judgment is described in Ezekiel.

> With might and fury I will bring you out from the lands where you are scattered. I will bring you into the wilderness of the nations, and there I will judge you face to face. I will judge you there just as I did your ancestors in the wilderness after bringing them out of Egypt, says the Sovereign LORD. I will count you carefully and hold you to the terms of the covenant. I will purge you of all those who rebel and sin against me. I will bring them out of the countries where

they are in exile, but they will never enter the land of Israel. And when that happens, you will know that I am the LORD (Ezekiel 20:34-38 NLT).

This judgment will purge out the rebels from among the nation. The non-rebellious will be the ones entering the kingdom.

Jesus also illustrated this judgment in Matthew 25:1-30 in the parables of the ten maidens and the ten talents. This judgment will be a separation of the saved and the lost of those from Israel. We can note the following.

A. THEY WILL BE REGATHERED FROM ALL OVER THE WORLD

These survivors of the Great Tribulation will be re-gathered from all over the world to the land of Israel. This will follow the victory of Christ over His enemies at the War, or campaign, of Armageddon.

B. THE PURPOSE OF THIS JUDGMENT: TO DETERMINE WHOM WILL ENTER THE KINGDOM

Jesus will cause them to "pass under my rod." The purpose is to determine which individuals will enter God's kingdom upon the earth, the Millennium. The righteous from Israel, those who have put their trust in Christ, will enter the kingdom of God. They will experience the long-promised blessings that God has given to that nation. These believers will enter into the millennial kingdom with earthly bodies, not resurrected or glorified bodies.

C. THE UNRIGHTEOUS WILL BE SENT AWAY

However, not everyone will enter the kingdom. The unrighteous from the nation will be purged from the righteous and sent away to punishment. Jesus illustrated this truth in the parable of the talents. He said.

And throw this good-for-nothing slave into the outer darkness. In that place there will be weeping and gnashing of teeth (Matthew 25:30 HCSB).

They will be banished from the presence of God.

D. THEY WILL AWAIT FINAL JUDGMENT

Although the Scripture does not say, it seems that these people will probably be put to death at that time. Their final judgment does not take place on this occasion. It will most-likely occur after the Millennium, the thousand year reign of Jesus Christ upon the earth. They, along will all other unbelievers which have ever lived, will be judged at that time.

This briefly sums up what will happen to those from the nation of Israel when Jesus Christ returns. There is a judgment waiting for them.

GROUP 2: THE LIVING GENTILE NATIONS ARE JUDGED

Jesus spoke of judging the living Gentile (non-Jewish) nations at His Second Coming. Matthew records Jesus saying the following.

> When the Son of Man comes in his glory with all of his angels, he will sit on his royal throne. The people of all nations will be brought before him, and he will separate them, as shepherds separate their sheep from their goats (Matthew 25:31,32 CEV).

Individuals from all the nations will be gathered for judgment at that time.

A. THOSE SURVIVING THE GREAT TRIBULATION WILL BE JUDGED

These Gentiles are people who are still upon the earth at the end of the Great Tribulation period, the seventieth week of Daniel. This refers to the final seven-year period which the earth will experience before the return of Christ.

These particular Gentiles are the living, not the dead. The dead will be raised for the purpose of judgment in the future. The prophet Isaiah wrote of these people from the Gentile nations in the following manner.

> To the LORD, all nations are merely a drop in a bucket or
> dust on balance scales; all of the islands are but a handful

of sand. The cattle on Lebanon's mountains would not be enough to offer as a sacrifice to God, and the trees would not be enough for the fire. God thinks of the nations as far less than nothing (Isaiah 40:15-17 CEV).

Everyone who survives this terrible time will be judged.

B. THE PLACE IS STATED: JERUSALEM

They will be brought to the city of Jerusalem and judged in the valley of Jehoshaphat. We read in the Book of Joel.

> "At that time, when I restore the prosperity of Judah and Jerusalem," says the LORD, "I will gather the armies of the world into the valley of Jehoshaphat. There I will judge them for harming my people, for scattering my inheritance among the nations, and for dividing up my land. They cast lots to decide which of my people would be their slaves. They traded young boys for prostitutes and little girls for enough wine to get drunk" (Joel 3:1-3 NLT).

The site of their judgment is certainly appropriate. Jerusalem, the place where Jesus took the penalty of the sins of the world upon Himself at the cross of Calvary, will be the place of God's judgment.

C. INDIVIDUALS WILL BE JUDGED

While it is called "the judgment of the nations" it is individuals that will be judged. Other passages speak of a judgment of individuals when Christ returns.

In the parable of the wheat and the weeds Jesus put it this way.

> Let both grow together until the harvest. Then I will tell the harvesters to sort out the weeds and burn them and to put the wheat in the barn (Matthew 13:30 NLT).

Individual judgment is also illustrated in Jesus' parable of the good and the bad fish. Matthew records Jesus saying the following.

> Once again, the kingdom of heaven is like a net that was let down into the lake and caught all kinds of fish. When it was full, the fishermen pulled it up on the shore. Then they sat down and collected the good fish in baskets, but threw the bad away. This is how it will be at the end of the age. The angels will come and separate the wicked from the righteous and throw them into the blazing furnace, where there will be weeping and gnashing of teeth (Matthew 13:47-50 NIV).

Each person, from every Gentile nation, will be answerable to God.

D. THE RIGHTEOUS ENTER THE KINGDOM: UNBELIEVERS ARE SENT AWAY

The righteous will enter into God's millennial kingdom while the unrighteous will be taken to judgment. These Gentile unbelievers will be sent to the lake of fire. The King in Jesus' parable declared the following.

> Then the king will say to those on his left, 'Get away from me! God has cursed you! Go into everlasting fire that was prepared for the devil and his angels' (Matthew 25:41 God's Word).

It is not clear if these Gentile unbelievers are immediately sent to the lake of fire. Some think these unbelievers are killed at this point. They will be raised at the Great White Throne judgment and then sent to the lake of fire.

It could be argued that this is their final judgment so they do not have to appear at the Great White Throne judgment. Therefore, they are immediately thrown into the lake of fire. There is not enough information to be certain.

GROUP 3: THE TRIBULATION SAINTS

There will be people who will put their faith in Jesus Christ during the Great Tribulation period. Many of them will be killed. When Christ returns, those who became believers and were killed during this specific period of time will also be judged. They will be raised from the dead in a resurrected glorified body, receive rewards, and will enter into the kingdom of God.

In the Book of Revelation we read the following.

> I saw thrones, and those who sat on them were allowed to judge. Then I saw the souls of those whose heads had been cut off because of their testimony about Jesus and because of the word of God. They had not worshiped the beast or its statue and were not branded on their foreheads or hands. They lived and ruled with Christ for 1,000 years. The rest of the dead did not live until the 1,000 years ended (Revelation 20:4-6 God's Word).

These are the people who have been beheaded for the testimony of Jesus. They are in a different category from other believers.

GROUP 4: THE OLD TESTAMENT SAINTS

There will also be a judgment of the Old Testament saints. This refers to people who lived during the Old Testament period and trusted the Lord, the God of Israel. They will be raised from the dead and judged. Daniel wrote.

> Many of those who lie dead in the ground will rise from death. Some of them will be given eternal life, and others will receive nothing but eternal shame and disgrace (Daniel 12:2 CEV).

While Daniel speaks of both the saved in the lost being raised, it seems that only the Old Testament saints are raised at this time. The unbelievers from the Old Testament period will be raised and judged at the Great White Throne judgment.

The promise of judgment found here in the Book of Daniel is only a general statement of judgment for the saved and the lost. In other words, he does not specify if they are judged together or separate.

Jesus also spoke of this judgment. Matthew records Him saying.

> For I, the Son of Man, will come in the glory of my Father with his angels and will judge all people according to their deeds (Matthew 16:27 NLT).

These believers, who lived in the Old Testament period, will experience God's rewards.

THERE ARE THOSE WHO HAVE A DIFFERENT VIEW

It is important to note that this view of the judgment to come is not shared by every Bible-believer. We need to make the following observations about other perspectives.

A. NOT EVERYONE BELIEVES IN A SEPARATE JUDGMENT

Not everyone believes in a separate judgment of the nations from the Great White Throne judgment. They see only one final judgment at the end of time. In other words, there will be a "Judgment Day." Everything will take place on this one particular day.

B. NOT ALL AGREE ON THE EXISTENCE OF A LITERAL MILLENNIUM

Those who hold the view of only one final judgment are not in agreement with respect to the existence of the subject of the Millennium, the thousand year rule of Jesus Christ upon the earth. Some believe that a literal Millennium will occur while others do not. The views can be simply stated as follows.

VIEW 1: THERE IS ONE GENERAL JUDGMENT WHEN CHRIST RETURNS

There are many Christians who do not believe in a literal Millennium. They see only one general resurrection at the time of the Second Coming of Christ. All people who have ever been born, both the righteous and unrighteous, will be raised and then judged at this final judgment. There will be no separate judgment of the saved and the lost. In other words, there will be no intermediate earthly kingdom upon the return of Christ. Eternity will begin immediately after the "day of judgment."

VIEW 2: THERE IS ONE GENERAL JUDGMENT AFTER A LITERAL MILLENNIUM

There are others who do believe in a literal Millennium, but see only one judgment at the end of this thousand year period. They believe that there will be no judgment before Christ comes or even when He comes again. It is only *after* the thousand year period of the Millennium that everyone, from the beginning of time, will be judged.

ALL BELIEVERS AGREE THAT ALL HUMANITY WILL BE JUDGED BY GOD

All Christians agree that everyone, both the righteous and unrighteous, will be judged by God in the future. The righteous will go away into eternal life while the unrighteous will be eternally separated from God. The only difference among Bible-believers is the timing of these judgments, not the fact of these judgments. The coming judgment is certain!

SUMMARY TO QUESTION 31
WHOM WILL CHRIST JUDGE AT HIS SECOND COMING? (THE JUDGMENT OF THE NATIONS)

There are differences of opinion among Bible-believers as to the exact sequence of events when Jesus Christ returns to the earth. We will explain the premillennial view of coming events as well as note other perspectives.

The premillennial view of the future believes that there will be a literal one thousand year reign of Jesus Christ upon the earth after His return to our world. Therefore, Jesus returns to earth, pre, or before, that thousand year reign, or Millennium, begins. At His return Jesus will set up an intermediate earthly kingdom where He will rule from the city of Jerusalem. This will fulfill many of the promises to the nation of Israel which are found in the Old Testament.

At the end of the thousand-year reign, there will be a "Last Judgment" where all the unbelieving dead from all time are judged. After this occurs, a new heaven and new earth are created which will be inhabited by believers only. This sums up the premillennial view of future events.

According to this perspective, when Jesus comes to earth for the second time, before He sets up His earthly kingdom, He will judge four different groups of people: the nation of Israel, the living Gentile or non-Jewish nations, the tribulation saints, those who have believed in Him during the Great Tribulation period, and the Old Testament saints.

When Jesus returns there will be both Jew and Gentiles alive on the earth. The Jews and Gentiles will be judged separately. Matthew 25 speaks of the judgment of the nations, or the living Gentiles. He will separate them as a shepherd separates sheep from the goats.

The sheep, the believers, will enter into His kingdom, while the goats, the unbelievers, will be sent away for punishment. These living Gentile believers at the time of Christ's Second Coming will enter into His earthly kingdom, the Millennium, in earthly bodies. They will enjoy the benefits of the promised kingdom

There will also be a judgment of living Jews, those from the nation Israel, when Christ returns. Many of them will have recognized that Jesus is the genuine Messiah. Thus, they will enter into the earthly kingdom which was promised to the nation in the Old Testament.

The unbelieving Jews, like the unbelieving Gentiles, will not enter the millennial kingdom but rather will be sent away for some type of punishment. Most likely, this means physical death because it seems that their final judgment, and then punishment, will not take place until the thousand year rule of Christ has ended.

There will also be people raised from the dead at the time of the Second Coming of Christ and the judgment of the nations. Those raised at this time will be believers only. This includes the Old Testament believers as well as the tribulation saints.

The Old Testament saints are those people who lived before the time of Christ. They trusted in God's Word and were thus promised entrance into His kingdom. The prophet Daniel spoke of those righteous people being awakened from their sleep. This speaks of the resurrection of their body. At that time their bodies are raised from the grave and reunited with their spirits.

A final group is the tribulation saints. They are made up of Jews and Gentiles who believe in Christ after the true believers, the church, have been taken from the earth by means of the rapture of the church. This particular group of people pays with their lives for their belief in Jesus Christ. These martyrs are raised at the time of the Second Coming of Christ.

The ones who are raised from the dead will enter the kingdom in glorified bodies. In other words, their bodies will differ from the living Jews and Gentiles who are entering the millennial kingdom. This is, general speaking, the premillennial view of future judgments.

As we mentioned, not everyone agrees with this premillennial view. Many Bible-believing Christians think there will be only one general judgment of humanity where everyone believer and unbeliever, will be judged at once. Some who hold this view think that Christ will judge everyone when He returns. Those holding this view reject the idea of an intermediate earthly kingdom, a Millennium.

Others, who do believe in a Millennium, think that this one judgment will not take place until after the thousand years is over.

It must be recognized that there are good Bible-believers who hold each of these viewpoints.

However, no matter what view is held with respect to the sequence of coming events, all Bible-believers acknowledge that Jesus Christ will judge the living and the dead and they will be divided into two groups. Those who have believed will spend eternity with Him while those who have not believed are already in a state of condemnation. This condemnation will continue for all eternity.

This sums up the various views of Bible-believers with respect to what will occur when Jesus Christ returns to the earth.

What Is The Last Judgment?
(The Great White Throne Judgment)

When the Bible speaks of the "Last Judgment," it is not similar to taking a final test to see whether we pass or fail. That type of judgment has already taken place. It occurs in this life. What we do with Jesus Christ in this life determines how we will be judged in the next.

Thus, this Last Judgment is the public recognition of decisions long-since made. The Bible tells us about this awesome event.

1. JESUS SAID ALL HUMANITY WILL BE JUDGED

The "Last Judgment" is also known as the "Great White Throne Judgment." Jesus spoke of the eventual judgment of all humanity.

> Don't be so surprised! Indeed, the time is coming when all the dead in their graves will hear the voice of God's Son, and they will rise again. Those who have done good will rise to experience eternal life, and those who have continued in evil will rise to experience judgment (John 5:28, 29 NLT).

There will be a resurrection which leads to life as well as one which leads to condemnation. Everyone, however, will be judged.

In the Old Testament, the prophet Daniel wrote of a judgment that would lead to "everlasting contempt" or "eternal shame and disgrace." He wrote.

> Many of those who lie dead in the ground will rise from death. Some of them will be given eternal life, and others will receive nothing but eternal shame and disgrace (Daniel 12:2 CEV).

Judgment will come to everyone.

2. JESUS WILL BE THEIR JUDGE

The Bible says that the Lord Jesus Himself will be the Judge. He said.

> Moreover, the Father judges no one, but has entrusted all judgment to the Son . . . And he has given him authority to judge because he is the Son of Man (John 5:22,27).

The claim of Jesus Christ is that He will be the One who will judge humanity.

3. THE PARTICIPANTS AT THE GREAT WHITE THRONE JUDGMENT (THE PREMILLENNIAL VIEW)

Bible-believers are not agreed as to who will participate in the Great White Throne Judgment. According to the premillennial view, there will be four groups of people who will be judged at this particular time. They are as follows:

A. The Unsaved Dead Of All Time

B. Satan

C. The Fallen Angels

D. The Millennial Believers

These are the four specific groups which will be judged at this future time.

THE PREMILLENNIAL VIEW SIMPLY STATED

The premillennial view basically says that Christ will return before the Millennium, His thousand year reign upon the earth. At that time, He sets up and earthly kingdom where He will rule from Jerusalem for one thousand years.

At the end of the thousand years, there will be a final judgment. However, most believers have already been judged long before this time. Their judgment consists not of condemnation but rather of rewards. They have been ruling with Christ in His earthly kingdom. It is only at the end of the thousand years that this final judgment occurs. Most of the participants in this judgment are unbelievers.

With this in mind, we can observe what Scripture says about this final judgment according to the premillennial view.

A. ALL OF WICKED HUMANITY WILL BE JUDGED

The Book of Revelation speaks of a final judgment of all the wicked who have ever lived. After the thousand years of peace upon the earth, there is a final rebellion of Satan that will be stamped out by God. John wrote about this as follows.

> And when the thousand years are ended, Satan will be released from his prison and will come out to deceive the nations that are at the four corners of the earth, Gog and Magog, to gather them for battle; their number is like the sand of the sea. And they marched up over the broad plain of the earth and surrounded the camp of the saints and the beloved city, but fire came down from heaven and consumed them (Revelation 20:7-9 ESV).

After this event, there is a final judgment of the wicked. John also wrote.

> And I saw a great white throne and the one sitting on it. The earth and sky fled from his presence, but they found no place to hide. I saw the dead, both great and small, standing before God's throne. And the books were opened,

including the Book of Life. And the dead were judged according to what they had done, as recorded in the books (Revelation 20:11,12 NLT).

The people judged at the Great White Throne will include all those who have rejected the message of God. They are raised at this final judgment.

The last judgment will not occur until death and Hades give up their dead. The Book of Revelation says.

Then the sea gave up its dead, and Death and Hades gave up their dead; all were judged according to their works (Revelation 20:13 HCSB).

These people are merely called "the dead." No one is named. This is in keeping with the rest of Scripture where the unbelieving dead are unnamed. While they do they exist, and are being punished, in one sense, they are treated as though they did not exist.

B. SATAN WILL BE JUDGED

Satan, the created spirit-being who became the devil, is also judged. The Bible specifies his judgment in the Book of Revelation. It says.

And the devil, who deceived them, was thrown into the lake of burning sulfur, where the beast and the false prophet had been thrown. They will be tormented day and night for ever and ever (Revelation 20:10 NIV).

His punishment occurs at this time.

C. EVIL ANGELS WILL BE JUDGED

Although the Bible does not specifically say that the evil angels will be judged at this time, Jesus said the lake of fire was prepared for them. We read of His words in Matthew where He said.

Then He will also say to those on the left, 'Depart from Me,
you who are cursed, into the eternal fire prepared for the
Devil and his angels!' (Matthew 25:41 HCSB).

Their punishment will come at some time, most likely at the Great
White Throne.

D. MILLENNIAL BELIEVERS WILL BE REWARDED

While all people who enter the Millennium will be believers, there will
be children born to these people during the one thousand year millennial reign of Christ on the earth. Judgment will also take place for these
individuals who are born during the millennial period. They will have
an opportunity to believe in Christ or reject Him.

Those who have believed during this period will likely be judged at the
Great White Throne. However, their judgment consists of rewards, not
punishment. They will enter into God's eternal kingdom.

4. EVERYONE WILL GIVE AN ACCOUNT FOR THEIR BEHAVIOR

At the Great White Throne Judgment, everyone will give an account of
their deeds. Jesus spoke of this awesome moment.

I tell you, on the day of judgment people will give account
for every careless word they speak (Matthew 12:36 ESV).

Every word ever spoken will be taken into account.

In another place, He said that all secrets will be revealed.

There is nothing covered that won't be uncovered, nothing
hidden that won't be made known. Therefore whatever you
have said in the dark will be heard in the light, and what you
have whispered in an ear in private rooms will be proclaimed
on the housetops (Luke 12:2,3 HCSB).

Nothing will be hidden in this judgment.

5. THIS IS JUDGMENT TO THEIR FINAL STATE

The Great White Throne is the "Final Judgment." Those who are judged are assigned to their final state. The Bible does not indicate any chance for belief after this final judgment. This is truly an awesome event!

NOTE: NOT EVERYONE BELIEVES IN A LITERAL MILLENNIUM

We should also note that not every Bible-believer accepts the idea that there will be a literal Millennium following the return of Christ. They believe the Great White Throne Judgment occurs when Christ comes again. It is the "Last Judgment" which the Bible speaks about; the one and only judgment for humanity and angels.

Again, we stress the fact that though there are disagreements among Bible-believers over the timing of the Great White Throne Judgment, all agree that it will indeed occur someday.

SUMMARY TO QUESTION 32
WHAT IS THE LAST JUDGMENT? (THE GREAT WHITE THRONE)

According to the premillennial view of the future, the Great White Throne Judgment, or the "Last Judgment," will happen at the end of the Millennium. This is a one-thousand year period in which Jesus Christ will personally rule upon the earth.

When the Lord Jesus returns to earth He then sets up His earthly kingdom. It is at the end of this period of one thousand years when the final judgment occurs.

The Bible pictures God as sitting on a huge white throne at this final judgment. Jesus Christ, God the Son, will be the Judge. Those judged at this particular time will include the created spirit-being who became the devil, Satan, his evil angels, all unbelievers who have ever lived, and those who have believed in Christ during the Millennium.

The righteous will remain with the Lord forever while the unrighteous, the lost, will be sent into a lake of fire where they will remain forever separated from the Lord and His goodness. They will suffer everlasting conscious punishment.

There are Bible-believers who do not believe in a literal thousand year reign of Christ on the earth. They see one final judgment for all humanity at the end of time; not just these select individuals and angels whom we have mentioned. According to this perspective every human being who has ever lived, as well as the devil and his angels, will be judged at this Last Judgment.

For those who do believe that Christ was reign for a literal thousand years upon the earth they assume that the following scenario will happen.

After the thousand year period of peace, the Millennium, there is a one final rebellion against God. Once the rebellion is crushed there is a final judgment of the wicked. Those at the Great White Throne judgment include all the unbelievers from the beginning of life here on the earth.

Satan will be judged at this time as well as his fallen angels.

There will also be believers who have trusted Christ during the millennial period. They will enter eternity with Him at this time.

The final judgment will culminate God's plan for this earth. After this judgment eternity begins.

While Christians may debate among themselves the timing of these judgments, there is no debate about the fact that judgment is coming and that everyone, whether human or angel will eventually be judged.

What Will Be The Results Of God's Final Judgment?

When God's final judgment is ultimately completed a number of things will be once and for all accomplished. This includes the following.

1. GOD ACCOMPLISHES HIS PLAN FOR PLANET EARTH

God's plan for time and eternity will be finally accomplished. All things that He planned and purposed for humanity on this earth are now completed. Nothing more needs to be done. Everything has been finished.

2. JUSTICE IS FINALLY SERVED

Since God's plan will be finished this means that every wrong will now be righted. The justice that did not take place here on earth will finally occur. Paul wrote to the Colossians about this principle. He said.

> But he who does wrong will be repaid for what he has done, and there is no partiality (Colossians 3:25 NKJV).

Justice will finally be done. For many, the long wait will be over.

A. ALL ACCOUNTS ARE SETTLED

All accounts will be finally settled. The Bible speaks of God opening up the books and settling all issues.

> And I saw the dead, great and small, standing before the throne, and books were opened. Then another book was

opened, which is the book of life. And the dead were judged by what was written in the books, according to what they had done (Revelation 20:12 ESV).

Humans will be held responsible for the deeds committed in this life. Everyone will be fairly judged.

B. WE DO NOT NEED TO TAKE VENGEANCE NOW

Therefore, it is not the responsibility of humans to take vengeance upon others. Indeed, this is the job of the Lord!

This is why Paul wrote the following to the Romans.

> Beloved, never avenge yourselves, but leave it to the wrath of God, for it is written, "Vengeance is mine, I will repay, says the Lord (Romans 12:19 ESV).

Consequently, when someone sins against us we are to forgive them and trust that God will right the wrong in His perfect timing. Vengeance is His job, not ours.

C. WE SHOULD BEHAVE AS CHRIST

Because justice will eventually occur, we should behave as Christ. Peter wrote about the example which Jesus has provided for us.

> He did not commit sin, and no deceit was found in His mouth; when reviled, He did not revile in return; when suffering, He did not threaten, but committed Himself to the One who judges justly (1 Peter 2:22,23 HCSB).

The Apostle John wrote something similar.

> Those who say that they live in him must live the same way he lived (1 John 2:6 God's Word).

He is our example. Consequently, it should be the desire of our heart to behave like Him.

3. THE MINISTRY OF JESUS CHRIST IS COMPLETE

The ministry of Jesus Christ will have been completed. All things, which He set out to do, are now accomplished. When He came the first time, He completed the work that God the Father had given Him.

Indeed, on the night of His betrayal, Jesus prayed the following words to God the Father.

> I glorified you on earth, having accomplished the work that you gave me to do (John 17:5 ESV).

The work of Jesus was accomplished.

In addition, when He was about to die the following occurred.

> A jar full of sour wine stood there, so they put a sponge full of the sour wine on a hyssop branch and held it to his mouth. When Jesus had received the sour wine, he said, "It is finished," and he bowed his head and gave up his spirit (John 19:29,30 ESV).

Jesus stated publicly that He finished the work; salvation has been provided!

However there were other things to accomplish. These things will all be completed at the "Last Judgment."

4. THE GOAL OF HISTORY IS MET

The Paradise that was lost in the Garden of Eden, as recorded in the Book of Genesis, will be regained. Sin will be no more and righteousness will be everywhere. History will reach its goal. The old heaven and earth will pass away and a new heaven and new earth will be created.

The Christian can look forward to an eternity with the God of the Bible, the living God. What a wonderful future we have to look forward to as believers in Jesus Christ!

SUMMARY TO QUESTION 33
WHAT WILL BE THE RESULTS OF GOD'S FINAL JUDGMENT?

The Bible makes it clear that there will be a final judgment. This judgment will result in a number of things.

First, God's eternal plan for the world will be accomplished. Nothing more needs to be done. Everything which He planned and purposed for time and eternity will now have come to pass.

In addition, justice will finally be served. All injustices will be made right and all accounts will be settled. All humans will be held responsible for their actions and fairly judged by the One who knows all things.

Realizing this, the Christian can allow the Lord to avenge them rather than taking vengeance into their own hands.

Furthermore, the ministry of Jesus Christ will be once and for all complete. When He came the first time He finished the work that God had given Him to do.

However, there was still more to be done. This necessitates a Second Coming to the earth. After that there is the "Last Judgment." The final judgment will serve as a completion to His ministry.

Also, the goal of history will finally be met. Sin will be done away and righteousness will be everywhere. The old heaven and earth will pass away. All things will be made new.

This is the wonderful future the Bible lays out for those who believe in Jesus. Hopefully, everyone reading this will be part of that future.

What Observations And Conclusions Should We Make About The Resurrection Of The Dead And The Coming Biblical Judgments?

After looking at what the Bible has to say about the subjects of the resurrection of the dead, and the coming Biblical judgments, we can make a number of general observations and conclusions. They are as follows.

OBSERVATION 1: THE DEAD WILL BE RAISED BY THE LIVING GOD

There will be a resurrection of every human being who has ever lived and died. There will be no exceptions. This resurrection will be accomplished by the miraculous work of the God of the Bible. He is the only being who has this ability to raise the dead.

OBSERVATION 2: THE DEAD WILL BE RAISED AT DIFFERENT TIMES

While everyone who has died will be raised from the dead, this will not take place at the same time. Indeed, there are a number of resurrections which will occur over a span of time. The righteous will be raised at different times from the unrighteous.

OBSERVATION 3: EVERY HUMAN BEING WILL BE JUDGED

Every human being will be raised for the purpose of judgment. Indeed, in Scripture, the resurrection of the dead is always linked with judgment. Again, there are no exceptions to this. Everyone will be judged.

OBSERVATION 4: THE LORD WILL FAIRLY JUDGE EVERYONE

The Lord, the God of the Bible, will be the righteous judge. He will judge everyone with fairness. In other words, there will be no complaints from anyone that they were judged unfairly.

OBSERVATION 5: BELIEVERS WILL BE JUDGED DIFFERENTLY THAN UNBELIEVERS

While everyone will be judged, the judgment for believers is not one of condemnation, but rather one of rewards. Therefore, for the believers, judgment day is "reward day." Unfortunately, the judgment for the unrighteous is one of condemnation.

OBSERVATION 6: EVERY HUMAN WILL GO TO ONE OF TWO DESTINATIONS

As a result of His perfect judgment, every human being will go to one of two destinations. The believers will be with the Lord forever while the unbelievers will be banished from His presence. In other words, it is heaven for the believers and hell for the unbelievers.

OBSERVATION 7: TO GO TO HEAVEN, ONE MUST TRUST JESUS CHRIST AS THEIR SAVIOR

Scripture says there is only one way, one path, to get to heaven. This is through the person of Jesus Christ. He is the one way to reach the one God. There is no other way to get there.

OBSERVATION 8: OUR ETERNAL DESTINATION IS DETERMINED BY WHAT WE DO IN THIS LIFE

This final point cannot be overemphasized. The eternal destination of each and every one of us is decided in this life and in it alone. We do not have a second chance after death to determine our eternal destiny.

Consequently, a person must receive Jesus Christ as their Savior in this life if he or she is to enter the kingdom of heaven. After death, it is too late.

Therefore, it is crucial that each and every one of us accepts Christ while we have the opportunity. In fact, the Bible emphasizes that "now" is the time of salvation.

SUMMARY TO QUESTION 34
WHAT OBSERVATIONS AND CONCLUSIONS SHOULD WE MAKE ABOUT THE RESURRECTION OF THE DEAD AND THE COMING BIBLICAL JUDGMENTS?

From our look at what the Bible has to say about the subject of the resurrection of the dead and the coming judgments, we can make the following conclusions.

First, the dead will be raised in the future by the God of the Bible. This includes everyone who has ever lived and died.

All who are raised from the dead will be raised to judgment. While everyone will be judged, believers will be judged differently from unbelievers. Unbelievers will be condemned to punishment but the judgment of believers is one of rewards. Indeed, there is no condemnation for those who have trusted Jesus Christ. Consequently, judgment day for the believer is actually "reward day."

The Lord, the righteous Judge, will determine where people spend eternity. There are only two destinations where people will go: either in His presence or apart from Him. These two destinations are known as heaven or hell.

To go to heaven, one must believe in Jesus Christ as their Savior. Indeed, it is only through Jesus that a person can have entrance to heaven.

Finally, our eternal destination will be determined in this life and in it alone. Once we are dead our eternal destiny is fixed. There is no second chance to believe.

In sum, when we understand what the Bible has to say about the resurrection of the dead and the coming judgments, it becomes imperative that we trust Jesus Christ as our Savior. Indeed, He is our only hope for everlasting life in the presence of the Lord.

About The Author

Don Stewart is a graduate of Biola University and Talbot Theological Seminary (with the highest honors).

Don is a best-selling and award-winning author having authored, or co-authored, over seventy books. This includes the best-selling *Answers to Tough Questions*, with Josh McDowell, as well as the award-winning book *Family Handbook of Christian Knowledge: The Bible*. His various writings have been translated into over thirty different languages and have sold over a million copies.

Don has traveled around the world proclaiming and defending the historic Christian faith. He has also taught both Hebrew and Greek at the undergraduate level and Greek at the graduate level.

OUR NEXT BOOK IN THE AFTERLIFE SERIES:
VOLUME 4

Heaven

As we have seen, after the resurrection of the dead comes the judgment. The judgment of God leads people to one of two eternal destinations. Our next book in the series looks at the ultimate destination for believers, heaven. We will answer a number of important questions about heaven which include the following.

Does Heaven Actually Exist?

How Does A Person Go To Heaven?

Can Anyone Be Certain They Are Going To Heaven?

Will We See God In Heaven?

Will We Recognize Our Love Ones In Heaven?